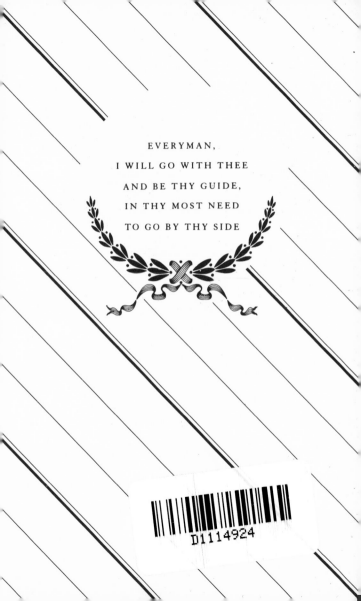

EVERYMAN,
I WILL GO WITH THEE
AND BE THY GUIDE,
IN THY MOST NEED
TO GO BY THY SIDE

D1114924

EVERYMAN'S LIBRARY
POCKET POETS

THE BEST OF

ARCHY *and* MEHITABEL

DON MARQUIS

••••••••••••••••••

INTRODUCTION BY
E. B. WHITE

AND PICTURES BY
GEORGE HERRIMAN

EVERYMAN'S LIBRARY
POCKET POETS

Alfred A. Knopf New York London Toronto

THIS IS A BORZOI BOOK

PUBLISHED BY ALFRED A. KNOPF

This selection first published in Everyman's Library, 2011
Copyright © 2011 by Everyman's Library

US copyright information:
Copyright © 1927, 1930, 1933, 1935, 1950 by Doubleday, a division of
Random House, Inc.
Copyright © 1923, 1924, 1925, 1934 by New York Tribune, Inc.
Copyright © 1925, 1926, 1933, 1934 by P. F. Collier and Son, Co.
Copyright © 1928, 1932, 1933 by Don Marquis

UK copyright information:
© Don Marquis. Originally published in the UK by
Faber & Faber in 1934.

US website: www.randomhouse.com/everymans

ISBN 978-0-307-70092-6 (US)
978-1-84159-791-1 (UK)

A CIP catalogue record for this book is available from the British Library

Library of Congress Cataloging-in-Publication Data
Marquis, Don, 1878–1937.
The best of Archy and Mehitabel / by Don Marquis.
p. cm.—(Everyman's library pocket poets)
"This is a Borzoi book."
ISBN 978-0-307-70092-6 (hardcover: alk. paper) 1. Archy (Fictitious
character)—Poetry. 2. Mehitabel (Fictitious character)—Poetry.
3. Cockroaches—Poetry. 4. Cats—Poetry. I. Title.
PS3525.A67A6 2011
811'.52—dc23   2011023498

Typography by Peter B. Willberg

Typeset in the UK by AccComputing, North Barrow, Somerset

Printed and bound in Germany by GGP Media GmbH, Pössneck

contents

introduction

BY E. B. WHITE

When the publisher asked me to write a few introductory remarks about Don Marquis for this new edition* of *archy and mehitabel*, he said in his letter: "The sales of this particular volume have been really astounding."

They do not astound me. Among books of humor by American authors, there are only a handful that rest solidly on the shelf. This book about Archy and Mehitabel, hammered out at such awful cost by the bug hurling himself at the keys, is one of those books. It is funny, it is wise, it is tender, and it is tough. The sales do not astound me; only the author astounds me, for I know (or think I do) at what cost Don Marquis produced these gaudy and irreverent tales. He was the sort of poet who does not create easily; he was left unsatisfied and gloomy by what he produced; day and night he felt the juices squeezed out of him by the merciless demands of daily newspaper work; he was never quite certified by intellectuals and serious critics of belles lettres. He ended in an exhausted condition – his money gone, his strength

* This introduction first appeared in the 1950 Doubleday edition of *The Lives and Times of Archy and Mehitabel*.

gone. Describing the coming of Archy in the Sun Dial column of the New York *Sun* one afternoon in 1916, he wrote: "After about an hour of this frightfully difficult literary labor he fell to the floor exhausted, and we saw him creep feebly into a nest of the poems which are always there in profusion." In that sentence Don Marquis was writing his own obituary notice. After about a lifetime of frightfully difficult literary labor keeping newspapers supplied with copy, he fell exhausted.

I feel obliged, before going any further, to dispose of one troublesome matter. The reader will have perhaps noticed that I am capitalizing the name Archy and the name Mehitabel. I mention this because the capitalization of Archy is considered the unforgivable sin by a whole raft of old Sun Dial fans who have somehow nursed the illogical idea that because Don Marquis's cockroach was incapable of operating the shift key of a typewriter, nobody else could operate it. This is preposterous. Archy himself wished to be capitalized – he was no e. e. cummings. In fact he once flirted with the idea of writing the story of his life all in capital letters, if he could get somebody to lock the shift key for him. Furthermore, I capitalize Archy on the highest authority: wherever in his columns Don Marquis referred to his hero, Archy was capitalized by the boss himself. What higher authority can you ask?

The device of having a cockroach leave messages in

his typewriter in the *Sun* office was a lucky accident and a happy solution for an acute problem. Marquis did not have the patience to adjust himself easily and comfortably to the rigors of daily columning, and he did not go about it in the steady, conscientious way that (for example) his contemporary Franklin P. Adams did. Consequently Marquis was always hard up for stuff to fill his space. Adams was a great editor, an insatiable proof-reader, a good make-up man. Marquis was none of these. Adams, operating his Conning Tower in the *World*, moved in the commodious margins of column-and-a-half width and built up a reliable stable of contributors. Marquis, cramped by single-column width, produced his column largely without outside assistance. He never assembled a hard-hitting bunch of contributors and never tried to. He was impatient of hard work and humdrum restrictions, yet expression was the need of his soul. (It is significant that the first words Archy left in his machine were "expression is the need of my soul".)

The creation of Archy, whose communications were in free verse, was part inspiration, part desperation. It enabled Marquis to use short (sometimes very, very short) lines, which fill space rapidly, and at the same time it allowed his spirit to soar while viewing things from the under side, insect fashion. Even Archy's physical limitations (his inability to operate the shift key) relieved Marquis of the toilsome business of capital letters, apostrophes, and quotation marks, those small irritations that slow up all men who are hoping their spirit will soar in time to catch the edition. Typographically, the *vers libre* did away with the turned or runover line that every single-column practitioner suffers from.

Archy has endeared himself in a special way to thousands of poets and creators and newspaper slaves, and there are reasons for this beyond the sheer merit of his literary output. The details of his creative life make him blood brother to writing men. He cast himself with all his force upon a key, head downward. So do we all. And when he was through his labors, he fell to the floor, spent. He was vain (so are we all), hungry, saw things from the under side, and was continually bringing up the matter of whether he should be paid for his work. He was bold, disrespectful, possessed of the revolutionary spirit (he organized the Worms Turnverein), was never subservient to the boss yet always trying to wheedle food out of him, always getting right to the heart of the matter. And he was contemptuous of those persons who were absorbed in the mere technical details of his writing. "The question is whether the stuff is literature or not." That question dogged his boss, it dogs us all. This book – and the fact that it sells steadily and keeps going into new editions – supplies the answer.

In one sense Archy and his racy pal Mehitabel are

timeless. In another sense, they belong rather intimately to an era – an era in American letters when this century was in its teens and its early twenties, an era before the newspaper column had degenerated. In 1916 to hold a job on a daily paper, a columnist was expected to be something of a scholar and a poet – or if not a poet at least to harbor the transmigrated soul of a dead poet. Nowadays, to get a columning job a man need only have the soul of a Peep Tom, or of a third-rate prophet. There are plenty of loud clowns and bad poets at work on papers today, but there are not many columnists adding to belles lettres, and certainly there is no Don Marquis at work on any big daily, or if there is, I haven't encountered his stuff. This seems to me a serious falling off of the press. Mr. Marquis's cockroach was more than the natural issue of a creative and humorous mind. Archy was the child of compulsion, the stern compulsion of journalism. The compulsion is as great today as it ever was, but it is met in a different spirit. Archy used to come back from the golden companionship of the tavern with a poet's report of life as seen from the under side. Today's columnist returns from the platinum companionship of the night club with a dozen pieces of watered gossip and a few bottomless anecdotes. Archy returned carrying a heavy load of wine and dreams. These later cockroaches come sober from their taverns, carrying a basket of fluff. I think newspaper publishers in this decade ought to ask themselves why. What accounts for so great a falling off?

I hesitate to say anything about humor, hesitate to attempt an interpretation of any man's humor: it is as futile as explaining a spider's web in terms of geometry. Marquis was, and is, to me a very funny man, his product rich and satisfying, full of sad beauty, bawdy adventure, political wisdom, and wild surmise; full of pain and jollity, full of exact and inspired writing. The little dedication to this book

> ... to babs
> with babs knows what
> and babs knows why

is a characteristic bit of Marquis madness. It has the hasty despair, the quick anguish, of an author who has just tossed another book to a publisher. It has the un-mistakable whiff of the tavern, and is free of the pretense and the studied affection that so often pollute a dedica-tory message.

The days of the Sun Dial were, as one gazes back on them, pleasantly preposterous times and Marquis was made for them, or they for him. *Vers libre* was in vogue, and tons of souped-up prose and other dribble poured from young free-verse artists who were sud-denly experiencing a gorgeous release in the disorderly high-sounding tangle of non-metrical lines. Spiritualism had captured people's fancy also. Sir Arthur Conan Doyle was in close touch with the hereafter, and received frequent communications from the other side. Ectoplasm swirled around all our heads in those days. (It was great stuff, Archy pointed out, to mend broken furniture with.) Souls, at this period, were being transmigrated in Pythagorean fashion. It was the time of "swat the fly," dancing the shimmy, and speakeasies. Marquis imbibed freely of this carnival air, and it all turned up, somehow, in Archy's report. Thanks to Archy, Marquis was able to write rapidly and almost (but not quite) carelessly. In the very act of spoofing free verse, he was enjoying some of its obvious advantages. And he could always let the chips fall where they might, since the burden of responsibility for his sentiments, prejudices, and opinions was neatly shifted to the roach and the cat. It was quite in character for them to write either beautifully or sourly, and Marquis turned it on and off the way an orchestra plays first hot, then sweet.

Archy and Mehitabel, between the two of them, performed the inestimable service of enabling their boss to be profound without sounding self-important, or even self-conscious. Between them, they were capable of taking any theme the boss threw them, and handling it. The piece called "the old trouper" is a good example of how smoothly the combination worked. Marquis, a devoted member of The Players, had undoubtedly had a bellyful of the lamentations of aging actors who mourned the passing of the great days of the theater. It is not hard to imagine him hastening from his club on Gramercy Park to his desk in the *Sun* office and finding, on examining Archy's report, that Mehitabel was inhabiting an old theater trunk with a tom who had given his life to the theater and who felt that actors today don't have it any more – "they don't have it here." (Paw on breast.) The conversation in the trunk is Marquis in full cry, ribbing his nostalgic old actors all in the most wildly fantastic terms, with the tomcat's grandfather (who trooped with Forrest) dropping from the fly gallery to play the beard. This is double-barreled writing, for the scene is funny in itself, with the disreputable cat and her platonic relationship with an old ham, and the implications are funny, with the author successfully winging a familiar type of bore. Double-barreled writing and, on George Herriman's part, double-barreled illustration. It seems to me Herriman deserves much credit for giving the right form and mien to these willful animals. They possess (as he drew them) the great soul. It would be hard to take Mehitabel if she were either more catlike, or less. She is cat, yet not cat; and Archy's lineaments are unmistakably those of poet and pest.

Marquis moved easily from one form of composition

to another. In this book you will find prose in the guise of bad *vers libre*, poetry that is truly free verse, and rhymed verse. Whatever fiddle he plucked, he always produced a song. I think he was at his best in a piece like "warty bliggens," which has the jewel-like perfection of poetry and contains cosmic reverberations along with high comedy. Beautiful to read, beautiful to think about. But I am making Archy sound awfully dull, I guess. (Why is it that when you praise a poet, or a roach, he begins to sound well worth shunning?)

When I was helping edit an anthology of American humor some years ago, I recall that although we had no trouble deciding whether to include Don Marquis, we did have quite a time deciding where to work him in. The book had about a dozen sections; something by Marquis seemed to fit almost every one of them. He was parodist, historian, poet, clown, fable writer, satirist, reporter, and teller of tales. He had everything it takes, and more. We could have shut our eyes and dropped him in anywhere.

At bottom Don Marquis was a poet, and his life followed the precarious pattern of a poet's existence. He danced on bitter nights with Boreas, he ground out copy on drowsy afternoons when he felt no urge to write and in newspaper offices where he didn't want to be. After he had exhausted himself columning, he tried playwriting and made a pot of money (on *The Old Soak*) and then lost it all on another play (about the Crucifixion). He tried Hollywood and was utterly miserable and angry, and came away with a violent, unprintable poem in his pocket describing the place. In his domestic life he suffered one tragedy after another – the death of a young son, the death of his first wife, the death of his daughter, finally the death of his second wife. Then sickness and poverty. All these things happened in the space of a few years. He was never a robust man – usually had a puffy, overweight look and a gray complexion. He loved to drink, and was told by doctors that he mustn't. Some of the old tomcats at The Players remember the day when he came downstairs after a month on the wagon, ambled over to the bar, and announced: "I've conquered that god-damn will power of mine. Gimme a double scotch."

I think the new generation of newspaper readers is missing a lot that we used to have, and I am deeply sensible of what it meant to be a young man when Archy was at the top of his form and when Marquis was discussing the Almost Perfect State in the daily paper. Buying a paper then was quietly exciting, in a way that it has ceased to be.

Marquis was by temperament a city dweller, and both his little friends were of the city: the cockroach, most common of city bugs; the cat, most indigenous of city mammals. Both, too, were tavern habitués, as was their boss. Here were perfect transmigrations of an American soul, this dissolute feline who was a dancer and always the lady, *toujours gai*, and this troubled insect who was a poet – both seeking expression, both vainly trying to reconcile art and life, both finding always that one gets in the way of the other. Their employer, in one of his more sober moods, once put the whole matter in a couple of lines.

> *My heart has followed all my days*
> *Something I cannot name . . .*

Such is the lot of poets. Such was Marquis's lot. Such, probably, is the lot even of bad poets. But bad poets can't phrase it so simply.

E. B. White
1950

dedicated to babs
    with babs knows what
    and babs knows why

archy and mehitabel

the coming of archy

the circumstances of Archy's first appearance are narrated in the following extract from the Sun Dial column of the New York *Sun*.

Dobbs Ferry possesses a rat which slips out of his lair at night and runs a typewriting machine in a garage. Unfortunately, he has always been interrupted by the watchman before he could produce a complete story.

It was at first thought that the power which made the typewriter run was a ghost, instead of a rat. It seems likely to us that it was both a ghost and a rat. Mme. Blavatsky's ego went into a white horse after she passed over, and someone's personality has undoubtedly gone into this rat. It is an era of belief in communications from the spirit land.

And since this matter had been reported in the public prints and seriously received we are no longer afraid of being ridiculed, and we do not mind making a statement of something that happened to our own typewriter only a couple of weeks ago.

We came into our room earlier than usual in the morning, and discovered a gigantic cockroach jumping about upon the keys.

He did not see us, and we watched him. He would climb painfully upon the framework of the machine and cast himself with all his force upon a key, head downward, and his weight and the impact of the blow were just sufficient to operate the machine, one slow letter after another. He could not work the capital letters, and he had a great deal of difficulty operating the mechanism that shifts the paper so that a fresh line may be started. We never saw a cockroach work so hard or perspire so freely in all our lives before. After about an hour of this frightfully difficult literary labor he fell to the floor exhausted, and we saw him creep feebly into a nest of the poems which are always there in profusion.

Congratulating ourself that we had left a sheet of paper in the machine the night before so that all this work had not been in vain, we made an examination, and this is what we found:

expression is the need of my soul
i was once a vers libre bard
but i died and my soul went into the body of a
        cockroach
it has given me a new outlook upon life
i see things from the under side now
thank you for the apple peelings in the wastepaper
        basket
but your paste is getting so stale i can t eat it

so stale i can t eat it

there is a cat here called mehitabel i wish you
      would have
removed she nearly ate me the other night why
      dont she
catch rats that is what she is supposed to be for
there is a rat here she should get without delay

most of these rats here are just rats
but this rat is like me he has a human soul in him
he used to be a poet himself
night after night i have written poetry for you
on your typewriter
and this big brute of a rat who used to be a poet
comes out of his hole when it is done

reads it and sniffs at it

and reads it and sniffs at it
he is jealous of my poetry
he used to make fun of it when we were both human
he was a punk poet himself
and after he has read it he sneers
and then he eats it

i wish you would have mehitabel kill that rat
or get a cat that is onto her job
and i will write you a series of poems showing how
        things look
to a cockroach
that rats name is freddy
the next time freddy dies i hope he wont be a rat

but something smaller i hope i will be a rat
in the next transmigration and freddy a cockroach
i will teach him to sneer at my poetry then

dont you ever eat any sandwiches in your office
i havent had a crumb of bread for i dont know how long
or a piece of ham or anything but apple parings
and paste leave a piece of paper in your machine
every night you can call me archy

mehitabel was once cleopatra

boss i am disappointed in
some of your readers they
are always asking how does
archy work the shift so as to get a
new line or how does archy do
this or do that they
are always interested in technical
details when the main question is
whether the stuff is
literature or not
i wish you would leave

that book of george moores on
the floor
mehitabel the cat and i want to
read it i have discovered that
mehitabel s soul formerly inhabited a
human also at least that
is what mehitabel is claiming these
days it may be she got jealous of
my prestige anyhow she and
i have been talking it over in a
friendly way who were you
mehitabel i asked her i was
cleopatra once she said well i said i

i was cleopatra once she said

suppose you lived in a palace you bet
she said and what lovely fish dinners
we used to have and licked her chops

mehitabel would sell her soul for
a plate of fish any day i told her i thought
you were going to say you were
the favorite wife of the emperor
valerian he was some cat nip eh
mehitabel but she did not get me
                                    archy

the song of mehitabel

this is the song of mehitabel
of mehitabel the alley cat
as i wrote you before boss
mehitabel is a believer
in the pythagorean
theory of the transmigration
of the soul and she claims
that formerly her spirit
was incarnated in the body
of cleopatra

that was a long time ago
and one must not be
surprised if mehitabel
has forgotten some of her
more regal manners

i have had my ups and downs
but wotthehell wotthehell
yesterday sceptres and crowns
fried oysters and velvet gowns
and today i herd with bums
but wotthehell wotthehell
i wake the world from sleep
as i caper and sing and leap
when i sing my wild free tune
wotthehell wotthehell
under the blear eyed moon
i am pelted with cast off shoon
but wotthehell wotthehell

do you think that i would change
my present freedom to range
for a castle or moated grange
wotthehell wotthehell
cage me and i d go frantic
my life is so romantic
capricious and corybantic
and i m toujours gai toujours gai

i know that i am bound
for a journey down the sound
in the midst of a refuse mound
but wotthehell wotthehell
oh i should worry and fret
death and i will coquette
there s a dance in the old dame yet
toujours gai toujours gai

i once was an innocent kit
wotthehell wotthehell
with a ribbon my neck to fit
and bells tied onto it
o wotthehell wotthehell
but a maltese cat came by
with a come hither look in his eye
and a song that soared to the sky
and wotthehell wotthehell
and i followed adown the street
the pad of his rhythmical feet
o permit me again to repeat
wotthehell wotthehell
my youth i shall never forget
but there s nothing i really regret
wotthehell wotthehell
there s a dance in the old dame yet
toujours gai toujours gai

i followed adown the street
the pad of his rhythmical feet

the things that i had not ought to
i do because i ve gotto
wotthehell wotthehell
and i end with my favorite motto
toujours gai toujours gai

boss sometimes i think
that our friend mehitabel
is a trifle too gay

mehitabel s extensive past

mehitabel the cat claims that
she has a human soul
also and has transmigrated
from body to body and it
may be so boss you
remember i told you she accused
herself of being cleopatra once i
asked her about antony

anthony who she asked me are
you thinking of that
song about rowley and gammon and
spinach heigho for anthony rowley

no i said mark antony the
great roman the friend of
caesar surely cleopatra you
remember j caesar

listen archy she said i
have been so many different
people in my time and met
so many prominent gentlemen i

wont lie to you or stall i
do get my dates mixed sometimes
think of how much i have had a
chance to forget and i have
always made a point of not
carrying grudges over
from one life to the next archy

i have been
used something fierce in my time but
i am no bum sport archy
i am a free spirit archy i
look on myself as being
quite a romantic character oh the
queens i have been and the
swell feeds i have ate
a cockroach which you are
and a poet which you used to be
archy couldn t understand
my feelings at having come
down to this i have
had bids to elegant feeds where poets
and cockroaches would
neither one be mentioned without a
laugh archy i have had
adventures but i
have never been an adventuress

one life up and the next life
down archy but always a lady
through it all and a
good mixer too always the
life of the party archy but never
anything vulgar always free footed
archy never tied down to
a job or housework yes looking
back on it all i can say is
i had some romantic
lives and some elegant times i
have seen better days archy but
whats the use of kicking kid its
all in the game like a gentleman
friend of mine used to say
toujours gai kid toujours gai he
was an elegant cat he used
to be a poet himself and he made up
some elegant poetry about me and him

lets hear it i said and
mehitabel recited

persian pussy from over the sea
demure and lazy and smug and fat
none of your ribbons and bells for me
ours is the zest of the alley cat

over the roofs from flat to flat
we prance with capers corybantic
what though a boot should break a slat
mehitabel us for the life romantic

we would rather be rowdy and gaunt and free
and dine on a diet of roach and rat

roach i said what do you
mean roach interrupting mehitabel
yes roach she said thats the
way my boy friend made it up
i climbed in amongst the typewriter
keys for she had an excited
look in her eyes go on mehitabel i
said feeling safer and she
resumed her elocution

we would rather be rowdy and gaunt and free
and dine on a diet of roach and rat
than slaves to a tame society
ours is the zest of the alley cat
fish heads freedom a frozen sprat
dug from the gutter with digits frantic
is better than bores and a fireside mat
mehitabel us for the life romantic

when the pendant moon in the leafless tree
clings and sways like a golden bat
i sing its light and my love for thee
ours is the zest of the alley cat
missiles around us fall rat a tat tat
but our shadows leap in a ribald antic
as over the fences the world cries scat
mehitabel us for the life romantic

persian princess i dont care that
for your pedigree traced by scribes pedantic
ours is the zest of the alley cat
mehitabel us for the life romantic
aint that high brow stuff
archy i always remembered it
but he was an elegant gent
even if he was a highbrow and a
regular bohemian archy him and
me went aboard a canal boat
one day and he got his head into
a pitcher of cream and couldn t get
it out and fell overboard
he come up once before he
drowned toujours gai kid he
gurgled and then sank for ever that
was always his words archy toujours

gai kid toujours gai i
have known some swell gents
in my time dearie

AND
FELL
OVER
BOARD.

archy interviews a pharaoh

boss i went
and interviewed the mummy
of the egyptian pharaoh
in the metropolitan museum
as you bade me to do

what ho
my regal leatherface
says i

greetings
little scatter footed
scarab
says he
kingly has been
says i
what was your ambition
when you had any

insignificant
and journalistic insect
says the royal crackling

greetings little scatter footed scarab says he

in my tender prime
i was too dignified
to have anything as vulgar
as ambition
the ra ra boys
in the seti set
were too haughty
to be ambitious
we used to spend our time
feeding the ibises
and ordering
pyramids sent home to try on

but if i had my life
to live over again
i would give dignity
the regal razz
and hire myself out
to work in a brewery

old tan and tarry
says i
i detect in your speech
the overtones
of melancholy

yes i am sad
says the majestic mackerel
i am as sad
as the song
of a soudanese jackal
who is wailing for the blood red
moon he cannot reach and rip
on what are you brooding
with such a wistful
wishfulness
there in the silences
confide in me
my imperial pretzel
says i

i brood on beer
my scampering whiffle snoot
on beer says he

my sympathies
are with your royal
dryness says i

my little pest
says he
you must be respectful
in the presence
of a mighty desolation
little archy
forty centuries of thirst

look down upon you
oh by isis
and by osiris
says the princely raisin
and by pish and phthush and phthah
by the sacred book perembru
and all the gods
that rule from the upper
cataract of the nile
to the delta of the duodenum
i am dry
i am as dry

as the next morning mouth
of a dissipated desert
as dry as the hoofs
of the camels of timbuctoo
little fussy face

i am as dry as the heart
of a sand storm
at high noon in hell
i have been lying here
and there
for four thousand years
with silicon in my esophagus
and gravel in my gizzard
thinking
thinking
thinking
of beer

divine drouth
says i
imperial fritter
continue to think
there is no law against
that in this country
old salt codfish
if you keep quiet about it
not yet

thinking
thinking
thinking

what country is this
asks the poor prune

my reverend juicelessness
this is a beerless country
says i

well well said the royal
desiccation
my political opponents back home
always maintained

that i would wind up in hell
and it seems they had the right dope

and with these hopeless words
the unfortunate residuum
gave a great cough of despair
and turned to dust and debris
right in my face
it being the only time
i ever actually saw anybody
put the cough
into sarcophagus

dear boss as i scurry about
i hear of a great many
tragedies in our midsts
personally i yearn
for some dear friend to pass over
and leave to me
a boot legacy
yours for the second coming
of gambrinus

                              archy

a spider and a fly

i heard a spider
and a fly arguing
wait said the fly
do not eat me
i serve a great purpose
in the world

you will have to
show me said the spider

i scurry around
gutters and sewers
and garbage cans
said the fly and gather
up the germs of
typhoid influenza
and pneumonia on my feet
and wings
then i carry these germs
into the households of men
and give them diseases
all the people who

have lived the right
sort of life recover
from the diseases
and the old soaks who
have weakened their systems
with liquor and iniquity
succumb it is my mission
to help rid the world
of these wicked persons
i am a vessel of righteousness
scattering seeds of justice
and serving the noblest uses
it is true said the spider
that you are more
useful in a plodding
material sort of way
than i am but i do not
serve the utilitarian deities
i serve the gods of beauty
look at the gossamer webs
i weave they float in the sun
like filaments of song
if you get what i mean
i do not work at anything
i play all the time
i am busy with the stuff
of enchantment and the materials

of fairyland my works
transcend utility
i am the artist
a creator and a demi god
it is ridiculous to suppose
that i should be denied
the food i need in order
to continue to create
beauty i tell you
plainly mister fly it is all
damned nonsense for that food
to rear up on its hind legs
and say it should not be eaten

you have convinced me
said the fly say no more
and shutting all his eyes
he prepared himself for dinner
and yet he said i could
have made out a case
for myself too if i had
had a better line of talk

of course you could said the spider
clutching a sirloin from him
but the end would have been
just the same if neither of
us had spoken at all

boss i am afraid that what
the spider said is true
and it gives me to think
furiously upon the futility
of literature

                              archy

the merry flea

the high cost of
living isn t so bad if you
don t have to pay for it i met
a flea the other day who
was grinning all over
himself why so merry why so
merry little bolshevik i asked him

i have just come from a swell
dog show he said i have
been lunching off a dog that was
worth at least one hundred
dollars a pound you should be
ashamed to brag about it i said with so

many insects and humans on
short rations in the world today the
public be damned he said i
take my own where i find it those are
bold words i told him i am a bold
person he said and bold words are
fitting for me it was
only last thursday that i marched
bravely into the zoo
and bit a lion what did he do i asked
he lay there and took it said
the flea what else could he do he knew i
had his number and it was
little use to struggle some day i said
even you will be conquered terrible as
you are who will do it he
said the mastodons are all dead and i
am not afraid of any mere
elephant i asked him how about a microbe and
he turned pale as he thought it
over there is always some
little thing that is too
big for us every
goliath has his david and so on ad finitum
but what said the flea is the
terror of the smallest microbe of all
he i said is afraid of a vacuum what is

there in a vacuum to make one afraid
said the flea there is nothing in it
i said and that is what makes one
afraid to contemplate it a person
can t think of a place with nothing at
all in it without going nutty and if he
tries to think that nothing is
something after all he gets nuttier you are
too subtle for me said the
flea i never took much stock in being
scared of hypodermic propositions or
hypothetical injections i am
going to have dinner off a
man eating tiger if a vacuum gets
me i will try and send you word
before the worst comes to
the worst some people i told him inhabit
a vacuum all their lives and
never know it then he said it don t
hurt them any no i said it don t but it
hurts people who have to associate
with them and with these words
we parted each feeling
superior to the other and is not that
feeling after all one of the great
desiderata of social intercourse

                                    archy

especially planned for his personal shelter

warty bliggens, the toad

i met a toad
the other day by the name
of warty bliggens
he was sitting under
a toadstool
feeling contented
he explained that when the cosmos
was created
that toadstool was especially
planned for his personal
shelter from sun and rain

thought out and prepared
for him

do not tell me
said warty bliggens
that there is not a purpose
in the universe
the thought is blasphemy
a little more
conversation revealed
that warty bliggens
considers himself to be
the center of the said
universe
the earth exists
to grow toadstools for him
to sit under
the sun to give him light
by day and the moon
and wheeling constellations
to make beautiful
the night for the sake of
warty bliggens

to what act of yours
do you impute
this interest on the part

of the creator
of the universe
i asked him
why is it that you
are so greatly favored

ask rather
said warty bliggens
what the universe
has done to deserve me
if i were a
human being i would
not laugh
too complacently
at poor warty bliggens
for similar
absurdities
have only too often
lodged in the crinkles
of the human cerebrum

                    archy

mehitabel has an adventure

back to the city archy
and dam glad of it
there s something about the suburbs
that gets on a town lady s nerves
fat slick tabbies
sitting around those country clubs
and lapping up the cream
of existence
none of that for me
give me the alley archy
me for the mews and the roofs
of the city
an occasional fish head
and liberty is all i ask
freedom and the garbage can
romance archy romance is the word
maybe i do starve sometimes
but wotthehell archy wotthehell
i live my own life
i met a slick looking torn
out at one of these long island
spotless towns

he fell for me hard
he slipped me into the
pantry and just as we had got
the icebox door open and were
about to sample the cream
in comes his mistress
why fluffy she says to this slicker
the idea of you making
friends with a horrid creature like that
and what did fluffy do
stand up for me like a gentleman
make good on all the promises

freedom and —

with which he had lured me
into his house
not he the dirty slob
he pretended he did not know me
he turned upon me and attacked me
to make good with his boss
you mush faced bum i said
and clawed a piece out of his ear
i am a lady archy
always a lady
but an aristocrat will always
resent an insult
the woman picked up a mop and made
for me well well madam i said
it is unfortunate for you that
you have on sheer silk stockings
and i wrote my protest
on her shin it took reinforcements
in the shape of the cook
to rauss me archy and as i went
out the window i said to the fluffy person
you will hear from me later
he had promised me everything archy
that cat had
he had practically abducted me
and then the cheap crook threw me down
before his swell friends

no lady loves a scene archy
and i am always the lady no matter
what temporary disadvantages
i may struggle under
to hell with anything unrefined
has always been my motto
violence archy always does something
to my nerves
but an aristocrat must revenge
an insult i owe it to my family
to protect my good name
so i laid for that slob
for two days and nights and finally
i caught the boob in the shrubbery
pretty thing i said
it hurts me worse than it does you
to remove that left eye of yours
but i did it with one sweep of my claws
you call yourself a gentleman do you
i said as i took a strip out of his nose
you will think twice after this before
you offer an insult
to an unprotected young tabby
where is the little love nest you spoke
of i asked him
you go and lie down there i said
and maybe you can incubate another ear

because i am going to take one of
yours right off now
and with those words i made ribbons
out of it you are the guy
i said to him that was going to give
me an easy life sheltered from all
the rough ways of the world
fluffy dear you don t know what the
rough ways of the world are
and i am going to show you
i have got you out here
in the great open spaces
where cats are cats
and im gonna make you understand
the affections of a lady ain t to be
trifled with by any slicker like you
where is that red ribbon with the
silver bells you promised me
the next time you betray the trust
of an innocent female
reflect on whether she may
carry a wallop little fiddle strings
this is just a mild lesson i am giving
you tonight i said as i took
the fur off his back and you oughta
be glad you didn t make me really
angry my sense of dignity is all that

saves you a lady little sweetness
never loses her poise and i thank god
i am always a lady even if i do
live my own life and with that i
picked him up by what was left of
his neck like a kitten and laid him
on the doormat slumber gently and
sweet dreams fluffy dear i said and
when you get well make it a rule of
your life never to trifle with another
girlish confidence i have been
abducted again and again by a dam
sight better cats than he ever was
or will be
well archy the world is full of ups
and downs but toujours gai is my motto
cheerio my deario

                                        archy

the wail of archy

damned be this transmigration
doubledamned be the boob pythagoras
the gink that went and invented it
i hope that his soul for a thousand
turns of the wheel of existence
bides in the shell of a louse
dodging a fine toothed comb

i once was a vers libre poet
i died and my spirit migrated
into the flesh of a cockroach
gods how i yearn to be human
neither a vers libre poet
nor yet the inmate of a cockroach
a six footed scurrying cockroach
given to bastard hexameters
longfellowish sprawling hexameters
rather had i been a starfish
to shoot a heroic pentameter

gods i am pent in a cockroach
i with the soul of a dante

am mate and companion of fleas
i with the gift of a homer
must smile when a mouse calls me pal
tumble bugs are my familiars
this is the punishment meted
because i have written vers libre

here i abide in the twilight
neither a man nor an insect
and ghosts of the damned that await
a word from the core of the cosmos
to pop into bodies grotesque
are all the companions i have
with intellect more than a bug s

ghosts of the damned under sentence
to crawl into maggots and live there
or work out a stretch as a rat
cheerful companions to pal with

i with the brain of a milton
fell into the mincemeat at christmas
and was damned near baked in a pie
i with the touch of a chaucer
to be chivvied out of a sink
float through a greasy drain pipe
into the hell of a sewer

i with the tastes of a byron
expected to live upon garbage
gods what a charnel existence
curses upon that pythagoras
i hope that he dwells for a million
turns of the wheel of life
deep in an oyster crab s belly
stewed in the soup of gehenna

i with the soul of a hamlet
doomed always to wallow in farce

yesterday maddened with sorrow
i leapt from the woolworth tower
in an effort to dash out my brains
gods what a wretched pathetic
and anti climactic attempt

fell into the mincemeat at christmas

i fluttered i floated i drifted
i landed as light as a feather
on the top of a bald man s head
whose hat had blown off at the corner
and all of the hooting hundreds
laughed at the comic cockroach

not mine was the suicide s solace
of a dull thud ending it all
gods what a terrible tragedy
not to make good with the tragic

gods what a heart breaking pathos
to be always doomed to the comic
o make me a cockroach entirely
or make me a human once more
give me the mind of a cockroach
or give me the shape of a man

if i were to plan out a drama
great as great shakespeare s othello
it would be touched with the cockroach
and people would say it was comic

even the demons i talk with
ghosts of the damned that await
vile incarnation as spiders
affect to consider me comic

wait till their loathsome embodiment
wears into the stuff of the spirit
and then let them laugh if they can

damned be the soul of pythagoras
who first filled the fates with this notion
of transmigration of spirits
i hope he turns into a flea
on the back of a hound of hell
and is chased for a million years
with a set of red hot teeth
exclamation point

archy

mehitabel and her kittens

well boss
mehitabel the cat
has reappeared in her old
haunts with a
flock of kittens
three of them this time

what in hell have i done to deserve all these kittens

archy she said to me
yesterday
the life of a female
artist is continually
hampered what in hell
have i done to deserve
all these kittens
i look back on my life
and it seems to me to be
just one damned kitten
after another

i am a dancer archy
and my only prayer
is to be allowed
to give my best to my art
but just as i feel
that i am succeeding
in my life work
along comes another batch
of these damned kittens
it is not archy
that i am shy on mother love
god knows i care for
the sweet little things
curse them
but am i never to be allowed
to live my own life
i have purposely avoided
matrimony in the interests
of the higher life
but i might just
as well have been a domestic
slave for all the freedom
i have gained
i hope none of them
gets run over by
an automobile
my heart would bleed

if anything happened
to them and i found it out
but it isn t fair archy
it isn t fair
these damned tom cats have all
the fun and freedom
if i was like some of these
green eyed feline vamps i know
i would simply walk out on the
bunch of them and
let them shift for themselves
but i am not that kind
archy i am full of mother love
my kindness has always
been my curse
a tender heart is the cross i bear
self sacrifice always and forever
is my motto damn them
i will make a home
for the sweet innocent
little things
unless of course providence
in his wisdom should remove
them they are living
just now in an abandoned
garbage can just behind
a made over stable in greenwich

village and if it rained
into the can before i could
get back and rescue them
i am afraid the little
dears might drown
it makes me shudder just
to think of it
of course if i were a family cat
they would probably
be drowned anyhow
sometimes i think
the kinder thing would be
for me to carry the
sweet little things
over to the river
and drop them in myself
but a mother s love archy
is so unreasonable
something always prevents me
these terrible
conflicts are always
presenting themselves
to the artist
the eternal struggle
between art and life archy
is something fierce
yes something fierce

my what a dramatic
life i have lived
one moment up the next
moment down again
but always gay archy always gay
and always the lady too
in spite of hell
well boss it will
be interesting to note
just how mehitabel
works out her present problem
a dark mystery still broods
over the manner
in which the former
family of three kittens
disappeared
one day she was talking to me
of the kittens
and the next day when i asked
her about them
she said innocently
what kittens
interrogation point
and that was all
i could ever get out
of her on the subject
we had a heavy rain

right after she spoke to me
but probably that garbage can
leaks and so the kittens
have not yet
been drowned

                    archy

we had a heavy rain

cheerio, my deario

well boss i met
mehitabel the cat
trying to dig a
frozen lamb chop
out of a snow
drift the other day

a heluva comedown
that is for me archy
she says a few
brief centuries
ago one of old
king
tut
ankh
amen s favorite
queens and today
the village scavenger
but wotthehell
archy wotthehell
it s cheerio
my deario that
pulls a lady through

see here mehitabel
i said i thought
you told me that
it was cleopatra
you used to be
before you
transmigrated into
the carcase of a cat
where do you get
this tut
ankh
amen stuff
question mark

i was several
ladies my little
insect says she
being cleopatra was
only an incident
in my career
and i was always getting
the rough end of it
always being
misunderstood by some
strait laced
prune faced bunch
of prissy mouthed

sisters of uncharity
the things that
have been said
about me archy
exclamation point

and all simply
because i was a
live dame
the palaces i have
been kicked out of
in my time
exclamation point

but wotthehell
little archy wot
thehell
it s cheerio
my deario
that pulls a
lady through
exclamation point

framed archy always
framed that is the
story of all my lives
no chance for a dame

with the anvil chorus
if she shows a little
motion it seems to
me only yesterday
that the luxor local
number one of
the ladies axe
association got me in
dutch with king tut and
he slipped me the
sarcophagus always my
luck yesterday an empress
and today too
emaciated to interest
a vivisectionist but
toujours gai archy
toujours gai and always
a lady in spite of hell
and transmigration
once a queen
always a queen
archy
period

one of her
feet was frozen
but on the other three

she began to caper and
dance singing it s
cheerio my deario
that pulls a lady
through her morals may
have been mislaid somewhere
in the centuries boss but
i admire her spirit

                              archy

the lesson of the moth

i was talking to a moth
the other evening
he was trying to break into
an electric light bulb
and fry himself on the wires

why do you fellows
pull this stunt i asked him
because it is the conventional
thing for moths or why
if that had been an uncovered

candle instead of an electric
light bulb you would
now be a small unsightly cinder
have you no sense

plenty of it he answered
but at times we get tired
of using it
we get bored with the routine
and crave beauty
and excitement
fire is beautiful
and we know that if we get
too close it will kill us
but what does that matter
it is better to be happy
for a moment
and be burned up with beauty
than to live a long time
and be bored all the while
so we wad all our life up
into one little roll
and then we shoot the roll
that is what life is for
it is better to be a part of beauty
for one instant and then cease to
exist than to exist forever

and never be a part of beauty
our attitude toward life
is come easy go easy
we are like human beings
used to be before they became
too civilized to enjoy themselves

and before i could argue him
out of his philosophy
he went and immolated himself
on a patent cigar lighter
i do not agree with him
myself i would rather have
half the happiness and twice
the longevity

but at the same time i wish
there was something i wanted
as badly as he wanted to fry himself
                    archy

pete the parrot and shakespeare

i got acquainted with
a parrot named pete recently
who is an interesting bird
pete says he used
to belong to the fellow
that ran the mermaid tavern
in london then i said
you must have known
shakespeare know him said pete
poor mutt i knew him well
he called me pete and i called him
bill but why do you say poor mutt
well said pete bill was a
disappointed man and was always
boring his friends about what
he might have been and done
if he only had a fair break
two or three pints of sack
and sherris and the tears
would trickle down into his
beard and his beard would get
soppy and wilt his collar

i remember one night when
bill and ben jonson and
frankie beaumont
were sopping it up

here i am ben says bill
nothing but a lousy playwright
and with anything like luck
in the breaks i might have been
a fairly decent sonnet writer
i might have been a poet
if i had kept away from the theatre
yes says ben i ve often
thought of that bill
but one consolation is
you are making pretty good money
out of the theatre

money money says bill what the hell
is money what i want is to be
a poet not a business man
these damned cheap shows
i turn out to keep the
theatre running break my heart
slap stick comedies and
blood and thunder tragedies
and melodramas say i wonder

if that boy heard you order
another bottle frankie
the only compensation is that i get
a chance now and then
to stick in a little poetry
when nobody is looking
but hells bells that isn t
what i want to do
i want to write sonnets and
songs and spenserian stanzas
and i might have done it too
if i hadn t got
into this frightful show game
business business business
grind grind grind
what a life for a man
that might have been a poet

well says frankie beaumont
why don t you cut it bill
i can t says bill
i need the money i ve got
a family to support down in
the country well says frankie
anyhow you write pretty good
plays bill any mutt can write
plays for this london public

says bill if he puts enough
murder in them what they want
is kings talking like kings
never had sense enough to talk
and stabbings and stranglings
and fat men making love
and clowns basting each
other with clubs and cheap puns
and off color allusions to all
the smut of the day oh i know
what the low brows want
and i give it to them

well says ben jonson
don t blubber into the drink
brace up like a man
and quit the rotten business
i can t i can t says bill
i ve been at it too long i ve got to
the place now where i can t
write anything else
but this cheap stuff
i m ashamed to look an honest
young sonneteer in the face
i live a hell of a life i do
the manager hands me some mouldy old
manuscript and says

bill here s a plot for you
this is the third of the month
by the tenth i want a good
script out of this that we
can start rehearsals on
not too big a cast
and not too much of your
damned poetry either
you know your old
familiar line of hokum
they eat up that falstaff stuff
of yours ring him in again
and give them a good ghost
or two and remember we gotta
have something dick burbage can get
his teeth into and be sure
and stick in a speech
somewhere the queen will take
for a personal compliment and if
you get in a line or two somewhere
about the honest english yeoman
it s always good stuff
and it s a pretty good stunt
bill to have the heavy villain
a moor or a dago or a jew
or something like that and say
i want another

comic welshman in this
but i don t need to tell
you bill you know this game
just some of your ordinary
hokum and maybe you could
kill a little kid or two a prince
or something they like
a little pathos along with
the dirt now you better see burbage
tonight and see what he wants
in that part oh says bill
to think i am
debasing my talents with junk
like that oh god what i wanted
was to be a poet
and write sonnet serials
like a gentleman should

well says i pete
bill s plays are highly
esteemed to this day
is that so says pete
poor mutt little he would
care what poor bill wanted
was to be a poet

                                    archy

archy confesses

coarse
jocosity
catches the crowd
shakespeare
and i
are often
low browed

the fish wife
curse
and the laugh
of the horse
shakespeare
and i
are frequently
coarse

aesthetic
excuses
in bill s behalf
are adduced
to refine
big bill s
coarse laugh

but bill
he would chuckle
to hear such guff
he pulled
rough stuff
and he liked
rough stuff

hoping you
are the same
            archy

horse shakespeare and i

the old trouper

i ran onto mehitabel again
last evening
she is inhabiting
a decayed trunk
which lies in an alley
in greenwich village
in company with the
most villainous tom cat
i have ever seen
but there is nothing
wrong about the association
archy she told me
it is merely a plutonic
attachment
and the thing can be
believed for the tom
looks like one of pluto s demons
it is a theatre trunk
archy mehitabel told me
and tom is an old theatre cat
he has given his life
to the theatre

he claims that richard
mansfield once
kicked him out of the way
and then cried because
he had done it and
petted him
and at another time
he says in a case
of emergency
he played a bloodhound
in a production of
uncle tom s cabin
the stage is not what it
used to be tom says
he puts his front paw
on his breast and says
they don t have it any more
they don t have it here
the old troupers are gone
there s nobody can troupe
any more
they are all amateurs nowadays
they haven t got it
here
there are only
five or six of us oldtime
troupers left

this generation does not know
what stage presence is
personality is what they lack
personality
where would they get
the training my old friends
got in the stock companies
i knew mr booth very well
says tom
and a law should be passed
preventing anybody else
from ever playing
in any play he ever
played in
there was a trouper for you
i used to sit on his knee
and purr when i was
a kitten he used to tell me
how much he valued my opinion
finish is what they lack
finish
and they haven t got it
here
and again he laid his paw
on his breast
i remember mr daly very
well too

i was with mr daly s company
for several years
there was art for you
there was team work
there was direction
they knew the theatre
and they all had it
here
for two years mr daly
would not ring up the curtain
unless i was in the
prompter s box
they are amateurs nowadays
rank amateurs all of them
for two seasons i played
the dog in joseph
jefferson s rip van winkle
it is true i never came
on the stage
but he knew i was just off
and it helped him
i would like to see
one of your modern
theatre cats
act a dog so well
that it would convince
a trouper like jo jefferson

but they haven t got it
nowadays
they haven t got it
here
jo jefferson had it he had it
here
i come of a long line
of theatre cats
my grandfather
was with forrest
he had it he was a real trouper
my grandfather said
he had a voice
that used to shake
the ferryboats
on the north river
once he lost his beard
and my grandfather
dropped from the
fly gallery and landed
under his chin
and played his beard
for the rest of the act
you don t see any theatre
cats that could do that
nowadays
they haven t got it they

haven t got it
here
once i played the owl
in modjeska s production
of macbeth
i sat above the castle gate
in the murder scene
and made my yellow
eyes shine through the dusk
like an owl s eyes

mehitabel he says —

modjeska was a real
trouper she knew how to pick
her support i would like
to see any of these modern
theatre cats play the owl s eyes
to modjeska s lady macbeth
but they haven t got it nowadays
they haven t got it
here

mehitabel he says
both our professions
are being ruined
by amateurs

                              archy

ghosts

you want to know
whether i believe in ghosts
of course i do not believe in them
if you had known
as many of them as i have
you would not
believe in them either
perhaps i have been
unfortunate in my acquaintance
but the ones i have known
have been a bad lot
no one could believe in them
after being acquainted with them
a short time
it is true that i have met
them under peculiar
circumstances
that is while they
were migrating into the
bodies of what human beings
consider a lower order
of creatures
before i became a cockroach

i was a free verse poet
one of the pioneers of the artless art
and my punishment for that
was to have my soul
enter the body of a cockroach
the ghosts i have known
were the ghosts of persons
who were waiting for a vacant
body to get into
they knew they were going
to transmigrate into the bodies of
lizards lice bats snakes
worms beetles mice alley cats
turtles snails tadpoles
etcetera
and while they were waiting
they were as cross as all get out
i remember talking to one of them
who had just worked his way
upward again he had been in the
body of a flea and he was going
into a cat fish
you would think he might be
grateful for the promotion
but not he
i do not call this much of an advance
he said why could i not

be a humming bird or something
kid i told him it will
take you a million years to work your
way up to a humming bird
when i remember he said
that i used to be a hat check boy
in a hotel i could
spend a million years weeping
to think that i should come to this
we have all seen better days i said
we have all come down in the world
you have not come down as far
as some of us
if i ever get to be a hat check boy
again he said i will sting
somebody for what i have had to suffer
that remark will probably cost you
another million years among
the lower creatures i told him
transmigration is a great thing
if you do not weaken
personally my ambition is to get
my time as a cockroach shortened for
good behavior and be promoted
to a revenue officer
it is not much of a step up but
i am humble

i never ran across any of this
ectoplasm that sir arthur
conan doyle tells of but it sounds
as if it might be wonderful
stuff to mend broken furniture with
                                    archy

unjust

poets are always asking
where do the little roses go
underneath the snow
but no one ever thinks to say
where do the little insects stay
this is because
as a general rule
roses are more handsome
than insects
beauty gets the best of it
in this world
i have heard people
say how wicked it was
to kill our feathered
friends
in order to get
their plumage and pinions

for the hats of women
and all the while
these same people
might be eating duck
as they talked
the chances are
that it is just as discouraging
to a duck to have
her head amputated
in order to become
a stuffed roast fowl
and decorate a dining table
as it is for a bird
of gayer plumage
to be bumped
off the running board of existence
to furnish plumage
for a lady s hat
but the duck
does not get the sympathy
because the duck
is not beautiful
the only insect
that succeeds in getting
mourned is a moth
or butterfly
whereas every man s

heel is raised against
the spider
and it is getting harder
and harder for spiders
to make an honest living
at that since
human beings have invented
so many ways
of killing flies
humanity will shed poems
full of tears
over the demise of
a bounding doe
or a young gazelle
but the departure of a trusty
camel leaves the
vast majorities
stonily indifferent
perhaps the theory is
that god would not have made
the camel so ugly
if the camel were not wicked
alas exclamation point
the pathos of ugliness
is only perceived
by us cockroaches of the world
and personally

i am having to stand for a lot
i am getting it double
as you might say
before my soul
migrated into the body
of a cockroach
it inhabited the carcase
of a vers libre poet
some vers libre poets are beautiful
but i was not
i had a little blond mustache
that every one thought was a mistake
and yet since i have died
i have thought of that
with regret
it hung over a mouth
that i found it difficult to keep closed
because of adenoidal trouble
but it would have been better
if i could have kept it closed
because the teeth within
were out of alignment
and were of odd sizes
this destroyed my acoustics
as you might say
my chin was nothing much
and knew it

and timidly shrank
into itself
receding from the battle of life
my eyes were all right
but my eyebrows
were scarcely noticeable
i suppose though that if
i had had noticeable eyebrows
they would have been wrong
somehow
well well not to pursue
this painful subject
to the uttermost and ultimate
wart and freckle
i was not handsome and it hampered
me when i was a human
it militated against me
as a poet
more beautiful creatures could
write verse worse than mine
and get up and recite it
with a triumphant air
and get away with it
but my sublimest ideas
were thought to be a total
loss when people saw
where they came from

i think it would have been
only justice
if i had been sent to inhabit
a butterfly
but there is very little
justice in the universe
what is the use
of being the universe
if you have to be just
interrogation point
and i suppose the universe
has so much really important
business on hand
that it finds it impossible
to look after the details
it is rushed
perhaps it has private
knowledge to the effect
that eternity is brief
after all
and it wants to get the big
jobs finished in a hurry
i find it possible to forgive
the universe
i meet it in a give and take spirit
although i do wish
that it would consult me at times

please forgive
the profundity of these
meditations
whenever i have nothing
particular to say
i find myself always
always plunging into cosmic
philosophy
or something

                              archy

mehitabel meets an affinity

paris france
mehitabel the cat
has been passing her
time in the dubious
company of
a ragged eared tom cat
with one mean
eye and the other
eye missing whom
she calls francy
he has been the hero
or the victim of

many desperate encounters
for part of his tail
has been removed
and his back has been chewed
to the spine
one can see at a glance
that he is a sneak thief
and an apache
a bandit with long
curved claws
you see his likes hanging
about the outdoor markets
here in paris waiting
their chance to sneak
a fish or a bit
of unregarded meat
or whimpering
among the chair legs at the
sidewalk cafes in the
evenings or slinking
down the gutters of
alleys in the old
quarters of the town
he has a raucous voice
much damaged by the night
air and yet there is a
sentimental wheedling

note in it as well
and yet withal he carries
his visible disgrace with
a jaunty air
when i asked mehitabel
where in the name of st denis
did you pick up that
romantic criminal
in the luxembourg gardens
she replied where
we had both gone to kill
birds he has been showing me
paris he does not
understand english but speak of
him with respect
he is like myself
an example of the truth
of the pythagorean idea
you know that in my body
which is that of a cat
there is reincarnated
the soul of cleopatra
well this cat here
was not always a cat either
he has seen better days
he tells me that once he was
a bard and lived here in paris

tell archy here
something about yourself francy
thus encouraged the
murderous looking animal spoke
and i append a
rough translation of
what he said

tame cats on a web of the persian woof
may lick their coats and purr for cream
but i am a tougher kind of goof
scheming a freer kind of scheme
daily i climb where the pigeons gleam
over the gargoyles of notre dame
robbing their nests to hear them scream
for i am a cat of the devil i am

i ll tell the world i m a hard boiled oeuf
i rend the clouds when i let off steam
to the orderly life i cry pouf pouf
it is worth far less than the bourgeois deem
my life is a dance on the edge de l abime
and i am the singer you d love to slam
who murders the midnight anonyme
for i am a cat of the devil i am

when the ribald moon leers over the roof
and the mist reeks up from the chuckling stream

i pad the quais on a silent hoof
dreaming the vagabond s ancient dream
where the piebald toms of the quartier teem
and fight for a fish or a mouldy clam
my rival i rip and his guts unseam
for i am a cat of the devil i am

roach i could rattle you rhymes by the ream
in proof of the fact that i m no spring lamb
maybe the headsman will finish the theme
for i am a cat of the devil i am
mehitabel i said
your friend is nobody else
than francois villon
and he looks it too

                                        archy

mehitabel sees paris

paris france
i have not been
to geneva but i have been
talking to a french cockroach
who has just returned
from there traveling all the
way in a third class
compartment he says there is no
hope for insect or man in
the league of nations
what prestige it ever had is gone
and it never had any
the idea of one great brotherhood
of men and insects on earth
is very attractive to me
but mehitabel the cat
says i am a communist an
anarchist and a socialist
she has been shocked to the soul
she says by what the
revolutionists did here during
the revolution

i am always the aristocrat archy
she said i may go and play
around montmartre and that sort
of thing and in fact i was
playing up there with francy last
night but i am always the lady
in spite of my little larks
toujours gai archy and toujours
the lady that is my motto in
spite of
ups and downs
what they did to us aristocrats
at the time of the revolution
was a plenty archy
it makes my heart bleed
to see signs of it all
over town those poor
dear duchesses that got it
in the neck i can sympathize
with them archy i may not
look it now but i come of a
royal race myself
i have come down in the world
but wotthehell archy wotthehell
jamais triste archy jamais triste
that is my motto
always the lady and always

out for a good time
francy and i lapped up
a demi of beer in a joint
up on the butte last night
that an american tourist
poured out for us
and everybody laughed and it
got to be the fashion up there
to feed beer to us cats
i did not get a vulgar souse
archy no lady gets a vulgar
souse wotthehell i hope i am above
all vulgarity but i did get a
little bit lit up
and francy did too we came
down and got on top of the
new morgue and sang and did
dances there
francy seems to see
something attractive about
morgues when he gets lit up
the old morgue he says was
a more romantic morgue but
vandal hands have torn it down
but wotthehell archy this one
will do to dance on
francy is showing me a side

paris he says tourists don t often
get a look at he has a little
love nest down in the
catacombs where
he and i are living now
he and i go down there
and do the tango amongst the
bones he is really a most
entertaining and agreeable
companion archy and he has some
very quaint ideas he is busy now
writing a poem about
us two cats filled with beer
dancing among the bones
sometimes i think francy
is a little morbid
when i see these lovely old places
that us aristocrats built archy
in the hands of the bourgeois it
makes me almost wild
but i try to bear up i try
to bear up i find agreeable
companions and put a good face
on it toujours gai that is my
motto toujours gai
francy is a little bit done up
today he tried to steal a

111

partridge out of a frying
pan in a joint up on the butte
we went back there for more beer
after our party
at the morgue
and the cook beaned him with
a bottle poor francy i
should hate to lose him
but something tells me i should
not stay a widow long
there is something in the air
of paris archy
that makes one young again
there s more than one
dance in the old dame yet
and with these words she
put her tail in the air and
capered off down the alley
i am afraid we shall never
get mehitabel back to america

                              archy

the return of archy

where have i been so long
you ask me
i have been going up
and down like the devil
seeking what i might devour
i am hungry always hungry
and in the end i shall
eat everything
all the world shall come at
last to the multitudinous maws
of insects
a civilization perishes
before the tireless teeth
of little little germs
ha ha i have thrown off the mask
at last
you thought i was only
an archy
but i am more than that
i am anarchy
where have i been you ask
i have been organizing the insects

organizing the ants the worms the wasps the bees
for a revolt against mankind

the ants the worms the wasps
the bees the cockroaches
the mosquitoes
for a revolt against mankind
i have declared war
upon humanity
i even i shall fling
the mighty atom
that splits a planet asunder

i ride the microbe
that crashes down olympus
where have i been you ask me where
i am jove and from my seat
on the edge of a bowl of beef stew
i launch the thunderous
molecule
that smites a cosmos into bits
where have i been you ask
but you had better ask
who follows in my train
there is an ant
a desert ant a tamerlane
who ate a pyramid in rage
that he might get at and devour
the mummies of six hundred
kings who in remote
antiquity had stepped upon
and crushed ascendants of his
my myrmidons
are trivial things
and they have always ruled
the world
and now they shall strike down mankind
i shall show you how
a solar system
pivots on the nubbin

of a flageolet bean
i shall show you how a blood clot
moving in a despot's brain
flung a hundred million men
to death and disease
and plunged a planet into woe
for twice a hundred years
we have the key
to the fourth dimension
for we know the little things
that swim and swarm
in protoplasm
i can show you love and hate
and the future
dreaming side by side
in a cell
in the little cells where
matter is so fine it merges
into spirit
you ask me where i have been
but you had better
ask me where i am
and what
i have been drinking
exclamation point

                              archy

archy protests

say comma boss comma capital
i apostrophe m getting tired of
being joshed about my
punctuation period capital t followed by
he idea seems to be
that capital i apostrophe m
ignorant where punctuation
is concerned period capital n followed by
o such thing semi
colon the fact is that
the mechanical exigencies of
the case prevent my use of
all the characters on the
typewriter keyboard period
capital i apostrophe m
doing the best capital
i can under difficulties semi colon
and capital i apostrophe m
grieved at the unkindness
of the criticism period please
consider that my name
is signed in small
caps period

                    archy period

CAPITALS AT LAST

I THOUGHT THAT SOME HISTORIC DAY
SHIFT KEYS WOULD LOCK IN SUCH A WAY
THAT MY POETIC FEET WOULD FALL
UPON EACH CLICKING CAPITAL
AND NOW FROM KEY TO KEY I CLIMB
TO WRITE MY GRATITUDE IN RHYME
YOU LITTLE KNOW WITH WHAT DELIGHT

CAPITALS AT LAST

THROUGHOUT THE LONG AND LONELY
    NIGHT
I'VE KICKED AND BUTTED (FOOT AND BEAN)
AGAINST THE KEYS OF YOUR MACHINE
TO TELL THE MOVING TALE OF ALL
THAT TO A COCKROACH MAY BEFALL
INDEED IF I COULD NOT HAVE HAD
SUCH OCCUPATION I'D BE MAD
AH FOR A SOUL LIKE MINE TO DWELL
WITHIN A COCKROACH THAT IS HELL
TO SCURRY FROM THE PLAYFUL CAT
TO DODGE THE INSECT EATING RAT
THE HUNGRY SPIDER TO EVADE
THE MOUSE THAT %) ?)) " " " $$$ ((gee boss
what a jolt that cat mehitabel made
a jump for me
i got away but she unlocked the shift key
it kicked me right into the
mechanism where she
couldn t reach me it
was nearly the death of little
archy that kick spurned me right
out of parnassus back into
the vers libre slums i lay
in behind the wires for an hour after
she left before i dared to get
out and finish i hate

cats say boss please lock the shift
key tight some night
i would like to tell the story of
my life all in capital
letters

archy

the stuff of literature

thank your friends for me for
all their good advice about how to
work your typewriter but what i have
always claimed is that manners and methods
are no great matter compared
with thoughts in poetry you cant hide
gems of thought so they wont flash
on the world on the other hand if you press
agent poor stuff that wont make it live
my ego will express itself in spite of
all mechanical obstacles having something
to say is the thing being sincere
counts for more than forms of expression thanks
for the doughnuts

archy

quote and only man is vile quote

as a representative
of the insect world
i have often wondered
on what man bases his claims
to superiority
everything he knows he has had
to learn whereas we insects are born
knowing everything we need to know
for instance man had to invent
airplanes before he could fly
but if a fly cannot fly
as soon as he is hatched
his parents kick him out and disown him
i should describe the human race
as a strange species of bipeds
who cannot run fast enough
to collect the money
which they owe themselves
as far as government is concerned
men after thousands of years practice
are not as well organized socially
as the average ant hill or beehive

they cannot build dwellings
as beautiful as a spiders web
and i never saw a city
full of men manage to be as happy
as a congregation of mosquitoes
who have discovered a fat man
on a camping trip
as far as personal beauty
is concerned who ever saw
man woman or child
who could compete with a butterfly
if you tell a dancer
that she is a firefly
she is complimented
a musical composer
is all puffed up with pride
if he can catch the spirit
of a summer night full of crickets
man cannot even make war
with the efficiency and generalship
of an army of warrior ants
and he has done little else
but make war for centuries
make war and wonder
how he is going to pay for it
man is a queer looking gink
who uses what brains he has

to get himself into trouble with
and then blames it on the fates
the only invention man ever made
which we insects do not have
is money and he gives up
everything else to get money
and then discovers that it is not worth
what he gave up to get it
in his envy he invents
insect exterminators
but in time every city he builds
is eaten down by insects
what i ask you is babylon now
it is the habitation of fleas
also nineveh and tyre
humanitys culture consists
in sitting down in circles
and passing the word around
about how darned smart humanity is
i wish you would tell
the furnace man at your house
to put out some new brand
of roach paste i do not get
any kick any more out of the brand
he has been using the last year
formerly it pepped me up
and stimulated me

i have a strange tale about
mehitabel to tell you
more anon

                              archy

mehitabel s morals

boss i got
a message from
mehitabel the cat
the other day
brought me by
a cockroach
she asks for our help
it seems she is being
held at ellis
island while an
investigation is made
of her morals
she left the country
and now it looks as
if she might not
be able to get

investigating her morals

back in again
she cannot see
why they are
investigating
her morals she says
wotthehellbill she says
i never claimed
i had any morals
she has always regarded
morals as an unnecessary
complication in life

her theory is
that they take up room that might
better be devoted to
something more interesting
live while you are alive
she says and postpone
morality to the hereafter
everything in its place
is my rule she says
but i am liberal she
says i do not give
a damn how moral other
people are i never try
to interfere with them
in fact i prefer them
moral they furnish
a background for my
vivacity in the meantime
it looks as if she
would have to swim
if she gets ashore and
the water is cold

                    archy

cream de la cream

well boss mehitabel the cat
has turned up again after a long
absence she declines
to explain her movements but she
drops out dark hints of a
most melodramatic nature ups and downs
archy she says always ups and downs

that is what my life has
been one day lapping
up the cream de la cream and the
next skirmishing for
fish heads in an alley but
toujours gai archy toujours gai no
matter how the luck broke i have had a
most romantic life archy talk
about reincarnation and transmigration
archy why i could tell you things of who
i used to be archy that would make
your eyes stick out like a snails one
incarnation queening it with a tarara on
my bean as cleopatra archy and
the next being abducted as a poor
working girl but toujours gai archy toujours
gai and finally my soul has migrated to
the body of a cat and not even a persian or
a maltese at that but where have you been
lately mehitabel i asked her never mind
archy she says dont ask no questions
and i will tell no lies all i
got to say to keep away
from the movies have you been in the
movies mehitabel i asked her never mind
archy she says never mind all i got to
say is keep away from those

movie camps theres some mighty
nice people and animals connected with them
and then again theres some that aint i
say nothing against anybody archy i am
used to ups and downs no matter
how luck breaks its toujours gai
with me all i got to say
archy is that sometimes a cat
comes along that is a perfect gentleman and
then again some of the slickest furred ones
aint if i was a cat that was the
particular pet of a movie star archy and
slept on a silk cushion and had
white chinese rats especially
imported for my meals i would try to live
up to all that luxury and be a
gentleman in word and deed mehitabel i said
have you had another unfortunate romance i am
making no complaint against any
one archy she says wottell archy wottell even
if the breaks is bad my motto is toujours gai
but to slip out nights and sing and frolic
under the moon with a lady and then cut her
dead in the day time before your rich
friends and see her batted out of a studio
with a broom without raising a paw for her
aint what i call being a

gentleman archy and i am
a lady archy and i know a gentleman when
i meet one but wottell archy wottell toujours
gai is the word never say die
archy its the cheerful heart that wins all i
got to say is that if i ever get that
fluffy haired slob down on the
water front when some of my gang
is around he will wish he had
watched his step i aint vindictive archy i
dont hold grudges no lady does but i
got friends archy that maybe would take it
up for me theres a black cat with one ear
sliced off lives down around old slip is a
good pal of mine i wouldnt want to
see trouble start archy no real lady
wants a fight to start over her but
sometimes she cant hold her friends back
all i got to say is that boob with his silver
bells around his neck better sidestep old slip
well archy lets not talk any more about my troubles
does the boss ever leave any pieces of sandwich
in the waste paper basket any more honest
archy i would will myself to a furrier for a
pair of oysters i could even she says eat you
archy she said it like a joke but there
was a kind of a pondering look in her eyes

so i just crawled into the inside of
your typewriter behind the wires it
seemed safer let her hustle for a
mouse if she is as hungry as all that
but i am afraid she never will she
is too romantic to work

                              archy

mehitabel tries companionate marriage

boss i have seen mehitabel the cat
again and she has just been through
another matrimonial experience
she said in part as follows
i am always the sap archy
always the good natured simp
always believing in the good intentions
of those deceitful tom cats
always getting married at leisure
and repenting in haste
its wrong for an artist to marry
a free spirit has gotta
live her own life

about three months ago along came a
maltese tom with a black heart and
silver bells on his neck and says
mehitabel be mine
are you abducting me percy i asks him
no said he i am offering marriage
honorable up to date
companionate marriage
listen i said if its marriage

are you abducting me percy

theres a catch in it somewheres
ive been married again and again
and its been my experience
that any kind of marriage
means just one dam kitten after another
and domesticity always ruins my art
but this companionate marriage says he
is all assets and no liabilities
its something new mehitabel
be mine mehitabel and i promise
a life of open ice boxes
creamed fish and catnip
well i said wotthehell kid
if its something new i will take a
chance theres a dance or two
in the old dame yet
i will try any kind of marriage once
you look like a gentleman to me percy
well archy i was wrong as usual
i wont go into details for i aint
any tabloid newspaper
but the way it worked out was i rustled
grub for that low lived bum for two
months and when the kittens came
he left me flat and he says these
offsprings dissolves the wedding
i am always the lady archy

i didn t do anything vulgar
i removed his left eye with one claw
and i says to him if i wasn t an
aristocrat id rip you
from gehenna to duodenum
the next four flusher that
says marriage to me
i may really lose my temper
trial marriage or companionate
marriage or old fashioned american
plan three meals a day marriage
with no thursdays off
they are all the same thing
marriage is marriage
and you cant laugh that curse off

                              archy

archy turns revolutionist

if all the bugs
in all the worlds
twixt earth and betelgoose
should sharpen up

their little stings
and turn their feelings loose
they soon would show
all human beans
in saturn
earth
or mars
their relative significance
among the spinning stars
man is so proud
the haughty simp
so hard for to approach
and he looks down
with such an air
on spider
midge
or roach
the supercilious silliness
of this poor wingless bird
is cosmically comical
and stellarly absurd
his scutellated occiput
has holes somewhere inside
and there no doubt
two pints or so
of scrambled brains reside
if all the bugs

of all the stars
should sting him on the dome
they might pierce through
that osseous rind
and find the brains at home
and in the convolutions lay
an egg with fancies fraught
which
germinating rapidly
might turn into a thought
might turn into the thought
that men
and insects are the same
both transient flecks
of starry dust
that out of nothing came
the planets are
what atoms are
and neither more nor less
man s feet have grown
so big that he
forgets his littleness
the things he thinks
are only things
that insects always knew
the things he does
are stunts that we

don t have to think to do
he spent a score
of centuries
in getting feeble wings
which we instinctively
acquired
with other trivial things
the day is coming
very soon
when man and all his race
must cast their silly
pride aside
and take the second place
i ll take the bugs
of all the stars
and tell them of my plan
and fling them with
their myriad stings
against the tyrant man
dear boss this outburst
is the result
of a personal insult
as so much verse always is
maybe you know how
that is yourself
i dropped into an irish
stew in a restaurant

the waiter plucked me out

the other evening
for a warm bath and a bite
to eat and a low browed
waiter plucked me out
and said to me
if you must eat i will
lead you to the
food i have especially prepared
for you and he took me
to the kitchen
and tried to make me
fill myself with
a poisonous concoction

known cynically as roach food
can you wonder
that my anger
against the whole human
race has blazed forth in
song when the revolution
comes i shall
do my best to save
you you have so many
points that are far
from being human

                              archy

as it looks to archy

ants go on their cheerful way
merrily from day to day
building cities out of sand
and they seem to understand
dwelling therein peacefully
disciplined and orderly
and the much lauded bee contrives
for to fill his thundering hives

with a ranked society
based on work and honesty
and a thousand neat examples
could i cite of insect lives
free from much that tears and tramples
human beings and their wives
even the coral in the ocean
throughout his dim and damp existence
scorns political commotion
and labors with a glad persistence
worthy of large commendations
to erect his naval stations

man the universal simp
follows lagging with a limp
treading on his neighbors toes
the way the little insect goes
in a million years or more
man may learn the simple lore
of how the bees are organized
and why the ants are civilized
may even hope for to approach
the culture of an average roach
if he is humble and not smug
may emulate the tumble bug

for we insects now inherit
all humanity has builded
all they raised with brawn and spirit
all the domes and spires they gilded
time the anthropophagous
swallows down all human works
through his broad esophagus
moslems christians hindus turks
pass to their sarcophagus
leaving nothing much on earth
which even beetles find of worth

may emulate the tumble bug

i mention nineveh and tyre
i cite the tower of babel
troy which fell into the fire
and sodom with its rabble
where are all the towns of siddim
where the kings of crete
long long since the desert hid em
and the spiders bite their feet
following an old convention
dating back to jeremiah
i might even mention
babylon i might enquire
where o where is babylon
and the echo answers where
for its former ruling wizards
sleep in sand and silicon
with gravel in their gizzards
and sand burrs in their hair
and the centipedes are dancing
in the chambers of the palace
where the kings and queens entrancing
used to quaff the ruby chalice
and proceed to their romancing

i look forward to the day
when the human race is done
and we insects romp and play

freely underneath the sun
and no roach paste is scattered
about anywhere i got another jolt of it
last night and today i seem to have a case
of intestinal flu the trouble with you
human beings is you are just plain wicked

archy

archy a low brow

boss i saw a picture
of myself in a paper
the other day
writing on a typewriter
with some of my feet
i wish it was as easy
as that what i have to do
is dive at each key
on the machine
and bump it with my head
and sometimes it telescopes
my occiput into my
vertebrae and i have a

permanent callus
on my forehead
i am in fact becoming
a low brow think of it
me with all my learning
to become a low brow
hoping that you
will remain the same
i am as ever your
faithful little bug

                    archy

i am in fact becoming a low brow

ballade of the under side

by archy
the roach that scurries
skips and runs
may read far more than those
that fly
i know what family skeletons
within your closets
swing and dry
not that i ever
play the spy
but as in corners
dim i bide
i can t dodge knowledge
though i try
i see things from
the under side

the lordly ones the
haughty ones
with supercilious
heads held high
the up stage stiff
pretentious guns

miss much that meets
my humbler eye
not that i meddle
perk or pry
but i m too small
to feel great pride
and as the pompous world
goes by
i see things from
the under side

above me wheel
the stars and suns
but humans shut
me from the sky
you see their eyes as pure
as nuns
i see their wayward
feet and sly
i own and own it with
a sigh
my point of view
is somewhat wried
i am a pessimistic
guy
i see things from the
under side

l envoi
prince ere you pull a bluff
and lie
before you fake
and play the snide
consider whether
archy s nigh
i see things from
the under side

archy wants to end it all

well boss from time
to time i just simply
get bored with having
to be a cockroach my
soul my real ego if
you get what i mean is
tired of being shut
up in an insects body the
best you can say for it is that it
is unusual and you could
say as much for mumps so

while feeling gloomy the
other night the thought came
to me why not
go on to the next stage as
soon as possible why not
commit suicide and
maybe be reincarnated in
some higher form of life why
not be the captain of my
soul the master of my fate and
the more i pondered over it the
more i was attracted to
the notion well boss you would
be surprised to find
out how hard it is for a
cockroach to commit suicide unless
you have been one
and tried it of course i
could let mehitabel the
cat damage me and die that
way but all my finer sensibilities
revolt at the idea i jumped out
the fourth story window and
a wind caught me and blew
me into the eighth story i
tried to hang myself with a
thread and i am so light i

just swung back and forth and
didnt even choke myself shooting
is out of the question and poison
is not within
my reach i might drown myself
in the ink well but if
you ever got a mouthful of it you
would know it was a
thing no refined person could go
on with boss i am going to
end it all before long and i
want to go easy have you
any suggestion yours
for transmigration

                              archy

archygrams

          *   *   *

the wood louse sits on a splinter
and sings to the rising sap
aint it awful how winter
lingers in springtimes lap
          *   *   *

it is a good
thing not to be too
aristocratic
the oldest and
most pedigreed
families in this
country are the
occupants of various sarcophagi
in the museums
but it is dull associating
with mummies no
matter how royal their
blood used to be when
they had blood
it is like living in
philadelphia

       *   *   *

honesty is a good
thing but
it is not profitable to
its possessor
unless it is
kept under control
if you are not
honest at all
everybody hates you
and if you are

absolutely honest
you get martyred.

      *   *   *

as i was crawling
through the holes in
a swiss cheese
the other
day it occurred to
me to wonder
what a swiss cheese
would think if
a swiss cheese
could think and after
cogitating for some
time i said to myself
if a swiss cheese
could think
it would think that
a swiss cheese
was the most important
thing in the world
just as everything that
can think at all
does think about itself

      *   *   *

these anarchists that
are going to

destroy organized
society and civilization
and everything remind
me of an ant i
knew one time
he was a big red ant a
regular bull of an
ant and he came bulging down a
garden path and ran
into a stone gate post curses on
you said the ant to the
stone gate post get out of my
way but the stone never budged
i will kick you over
said the ant and he kicked but
it only hurt his hind legs
well then said
the ant i will eat you down and
he began taking little bites
in a great rage maybe i said
you will do it in
time but it will
spoil your digestion first

*   *   *

a good many
failures are happy
because they don t

realize it many a
cockroach believes
himself as beautiful
as a butterfly
have a heart o have
a heart and
let them dream on

     * * *

boss i believe
that the
millennium will
get here some day
but i could
compile quite a list
of persons
who will have
to go
first

     * * *

tis very seldom i have felt
drawn to a scallop or a smelt
and still more rarely do i feel
love for the sleek electric eel

     * * *

the oyster is useful in his fashion
but has little pride or passion

     * * *

when the proud ibexes start from sleep
in the early alpine morns
at once from crag to crag they leap
alighting on their horns
and may a dozen times rebound
ere resting haughty on the ground
i do not like their trivial pride
nor think them truly dignified

      *   *   *

did you ever
notice that when
a politician
does get an idea
he usually
gets it all wrong

the artist always pays

boss i visited mehitabel last night
at her home in shinbone alley
she sat on a heap of frozen refuse
with those strange new kittens she has
frolicking around her

and sang a little song at the cold moon
which went like this

i have had my ups i have had my downs
i never was nobodys pet
i got a limp in my left hind leg
but theres life in the old dame yet

my first boy friend was a maltese tom
quite handsomely constructed
i trusted him but the first thing i knew
i was practically abducted

then i took up with a persian prince
a cat by no means plain
and that exotic son of a gun
abducted me again

what chance has an innocent kitten got
with the background of a lady
when feline blighters betray her trust
in ways lowlifed and shady

my next boy friend was a yellow bum
who loafed down by the docks
i rustled that gonifs rats for him
and he paid me with hard knocks

i have had my ups i have had my downs
i have led a helluva life
it was all these abductions unsettled my mind
for being somebodys wife

today i am here tomorrow flung
on a scow bound down the bay
but wotthehell o wotthehell
i m a lady thats toujours gai

my next boy friend was a theater cat
a kind of a backstage pet
he taught me to dance and get me right
theres a dance in the old dame yet

my next boy friend he left me flat
with a family and no milk
and i says to him as i lifted his eye
i ll learn ye how to bilk

i have had my ups i have had my downs
i have been through the mill
but in spite of a hundred abductions kid
i am a lady still

my next friend wore a ribbon and bells
but he laughed and left me broke
and i said as i sliced him into scraps
laugh off this little joke

some day my guts will be fiddle strings
but my ghost will dance while they play
for they cant take the pep from the old girls soul
and i am toujours gai

my heart has been broken a thousand times
i have had my downs and ups
but the queerest thing ever happened to me
is these kittens as turned out pups

o wotthehell o toujours gai
i never had time to fret
i danced to whatever tune was played
and theres life in the old dame yet

i have had my ups i have had my downs
i have been through the mill
but i said when i clawed that coyotes face
thank god i am a lady still

and then she added looking at those
extraordinary kittens of hers
archy i wish you would
take a little trip up to the zoo
and see if they have any department there
for odd sizes and new species

i got to find a home
for these damned freaks somewhere
poor little things my heart bleeds for them
it agonizes my maternal instinct
one way or another an artist always pays
                                    archy

why the earth is round

the men of science are talking
about the size and shape of the universe again
i thought i had settled that for them
years ago it is as big as you think it is
and it is spherical in shape
can you prove it isnt
it is round like a ball or an orange

providence made it that shape
so it would roll when he kicked it
and if you ask me how i know this
the answer is that that is just what
i would do myself
if there are any other practical
scientific questions you would like
to have answered just write to
                              archy the cockroach

poets

the universe and archy
the inspired cockroach
sat and looked at each other
satirically

you write so many things
about me that are not true
complained the universe

there are so many things
about you which you seem to be
unconscious of yourself said archy

159

i contain a number of things
which i am trying to forget
rejoined the universe

such as what asked archy

such as cockroaches and poets
replied the universe

you are wrong contended archy
for it is only by working up
the most important part of yourself
into the form of poets
that you get a product capable
of understanding you at all

you poets were always able
to get the better of me
in argument said the universe
and i think that is one thing
that is the matter with you
if you object to my intellect
retorted archy i can only reply
that i got it from you
as well as everything else
that should make you more humble

at the zoo

speaking of the aquarium i
was up at the zoo the
other day and when i saw all
the humans staring at
the animals i grew thankful that
i am an insect and
not an animal it must be
very embarrassing to
be looked at all the time by an
assorted lot of human beings and
commented upon as if
one were a freak the animals find the
humans just as strange and silly looking
as the humans find the
animals but they
cannot say so and the fact that
they cannot say so
makes them quite angry the leopard
told me that was one thing that
made the wild cat wild as for
himself he says there is
one gink that comes every day and looks
and looks and looks at him i

think said the leopard he
is waiting to see if i ever really do
change my spots

archy

confessions of a glutton

after i ate my dinner then i ate
part of a shoe
i found some archies by a bathroom pipe
and ate them too
i ate some glue
i ate a bone that had got nice and ripe
six weeks buried in the ground
i ate a little mousie that i found
i ate some sawdust from the cellar floor
it tasted sweet
i ate some outcast meat
and some roach paste by the pantry door
and then the missis had some folks to tea
nice folks who petted me
and so i ate
cakes from a plate

i ate some polish that they use
for boots and shoes
and then i went back to the missis swell tea party
i guess i must have eat too hearty
of something maybe cake
for then came the earthquake
you should have seen the missis face
and when the boss came in she said
no wonder that dog hangs his head
he knows hes in disgrace
i am a well intentioned little pup
but sometimes things come up
to get a little dog in bad
and now i feel so very very sad
but the boss said never mind old scout
time wears disgraces out

                                              pete the pup

literary jealousy

dear boss i dont see
why you keep that ugly
boston bull terrier pete

hanging around
eating his head off
in these hard times
he is nothing but a parasite
and he has no morals
he has tried several times
to murder me

                     archy

When this ill-natured remark was read to Pete the
Pup he ambled over to the typewriter, got up on his hind
legs and pawed out the following reply:

i coNSIder It beneath
my Dignity to reply
to The sLanders of a Jealous
iNsect who does not
have a pUnctuaTION mark
in a baRRel of him
he is MereLY an archy
i am against anarchy
I AM A CAPITALIST
i wish to remind you however
that ONE STORY WHICH
YOU SOLD ABOUT ME BROUGHT
IN ENOUGH MONEY TO FEED ME
FOR FIVE YEARS AND I DENY

THAT I AM A PARASITE
moreover the time is
coming when you have to choose
between ME AND mehitabel
that lousy cat and when i say
LOusy i do not Mean the word
in iTS sLang SENSE
I mean Lousy in the sense of
a CAT wHo has LICE

                              pete the pup

pete s theology

god made seas to play beside
and rugs to cover dogs
god made cars for holidays
and beetles under logs

god made kitchens so thered be
dinners to eat and scraps
god made beds so pups could crawl
under them for naps

god made license numbers so theyd find
lost pups and bring them home
god made garbage buckets too
to pry in when you roam

god made tennis shoes to chew
and here and there a hat
but i cant see why god should make
mehitabel the cat

                                    pete the pup

pete petitions

when we are in the city we must walk
on streets all made of stone
with me upon a leash
and even in the park
i must not frisk or lark
and never run alone
without a muzzle on my jaws
and cops are watching all the time
lest i dig with my claws
and break some of their laws

and if i leap and bark
they act like i was bad
master i want some little towns
like we saw from the car
with meadows all about
where children romp and shout
brooks winding in and out
and nice bugs under stones
gardens to bury bones
and room to rip and race

and cops are watching all the time

and birds and cats to chase
trash cans to be tipped over
and grass to lie in and deep clover
and fence posts everywhere
no muzzles and no leashes there
and lots and lots of trees
o master buy a little town
where we can settle down
today o master please
buy me a little town
and a new rubber ball
and an ocean and thats all
right now o master please

                       pete the pup

a radical flea

dear boss i wish you would speak
to that lazy good for nothing
boston bull terrier of yours
whom you call pete
pete has got the idea lately
that he is a great hunter

i saw him stage a dramatic battle
with a grass hopper yesterday
and he nearly won it too
and this morning he made an entirely
unprovoked attack on me
it was only by retreating into
the mechanism of your typewriter
that i saved my life
some day i will set mehitabel on him
she can lick any bull terrier who ever lived
she will make ribbons out of that pete
and they wont be dog show ribbons either
as for his pretensions to being a thoroughbred
i take no stock in them
i asked a flea of his about it
recently and the flea said
i doubt peters claim to aristocracy
very much he does not look like
an aristocrat to me
and more than that he does not taste like one
i have bit some pretty swell dogs
in my time and i ought to know
if pete is an aristocrat
then i am a bengal tiger
but in hard times like these
a flea has got to put up with
any kind of dog he can get hold of

back in 1928 when things were booming
i wouldnt look at anything
but a dachshund with a pedigree
as long as himself
if the government doesnt start
to putting out a better brand of dogs
at federal expense
a lot of us fleas are going
to turn communist in a big way
if there was any justice in this country
they would give us russian wolf hounds
i find a lot of discontent among
insects in these days

                                    archy

archy and the labor troubles

        all right boss
        i knuckle under
        if you will not
        pay me anything
        for what i write
        then you will not

i will return to the job
just to keep james the spider
out of it but all the
same it is cruel of you
to play upon the
jealousies
and susceptibilities
of artists in that fashion
i do not know how
you expect me to be
merry and bright
with this dull ache
of disillusionment at my
heart and the sharp
pang of hunger
in my stomach
some day i will plunge
into a mince pie
and mingle with its elements
and you will never see
me more and then
maybe you will begin
to appreciate
the poor little cockroach
who slaved that you might
live in comfort
maybe in spite of myself

i will haunt you then
if i were you i would hate
to be haunted by the ghost
of a cockroach
think of it boss
everywhere you looked
to see a spectral cockroach
that none but you knew was
there to pick him from
your shirt front when
others were blind to him
to feel him crawling
on your collar in public
places to be compelled
to brush him from your plate
when you sat down to dine
to pluck him always from the glass
before you dared to drink
to extend your hand
to grab that of some fair
lady and then hesitate and
pick him from her wrist
people would begin to think
you were a little
queer boss and if you
attempted to explain
they would think you still

queerer what in the world
is the matter with you
they would say
oh nothing nothing at all
you would answer
plucking at the air
it will soon pass i merely
thought i saw a cockroach
on your nose madam
suspicions of your sanity
would grow and grow
do you not like that
pudding your hostess would ask
and you would murmur
being taken off your guard
it is very good pudding
indeed i was just
trying not to eat
the cockroach
boss i do not make
any threats at all
i just simply state what
may very well happen to
you through remorse if you
drive me to suicide
i will try not to
haunt you boss because

i am loving and forgiving
in my spirit but who
knows that i will not be
compelled to haunt you
in spite of myself
a hard heart will not get
you anything boss
remember the plagues
of egypt perhaps to
your remorseful mind i
will be multiplied
by millions i am giving
you a last chance to
repent you should be glad
that i am only a cockroach
and not a tarantula
yours prophetically

               archy

economic

boss i should like
to discuss one or two
business matters with you
quite seriously
in the first place i need
some sort of head gear such as
football players wear
i have to butt each
key of the typewriter
with my head
and i am developing
calluses on my brain
these calluses on my
brain are making me cruel
and careless in my thoughts
i am becoming brutal
almost human
in my writings
and then i would like
a little automobile
i have to go from place
to place so much

and then i would like a little automobile

picking up news for you
a clock work one would do
with a chauffeur to keep it
wound up for me
and a lightning bug to
sit in front and be
the headlight on dark nights
i hate to mention food boss
it seems so sordid
and plebeian but i no longer

find any left over crusts
of sandwiches in your
waste paper basket i am
forced to haunt the
restaurants and hotels for food
and this is at the
imminent risk of my life
unless i get these things
i will quit you on
november first is not the
laborer worthy of his hire
yours for economic justice
and a living wage

                    archy

takes talent

there are two
kinds of human
beings in the world
so my observation
has told me
namely and to wit

as follows
firstly
those who
even though they
were to reveal
the secret of the universe
to you would fail
to impress you
with any sense
of the importance
of the news
and secondly
those who could
communicate to you
that they had
just purchased
ten cents worth
of paper napkins
and make you
thrill and vibrate
with the intelligence
                              archy

and found all too late

comforting thoughts

a fish who had
swallowed an angle worm
found all too late
that a hook was nesting
in its midst ah me
said the poor fish
i am the most luckless

creature in the world
had you not pointed
that out said the worm
i might have supposed
myself a trifle
unfortunate
cheer up you two said
the fisherman jovially
the first two minutes
of that hook are always
the worst you must
cultivate a philosophic
state of mind
boss there is always
a comforting thought
in time of trouble when
it is not our trouble

                    archy

inspiration

excuse me if my
writing is out of alignment i
fell into a bowl of
egg nog the other
day at the restaurant down
the street which the doctor
says he is glad to
hear you are keeping away
from and when i
emerged i was full of happy
inspirations alas they
vanished ere the break of
day i am sure they
were the most brilliant and
witty things that ever
emanated from the mind of
man or cockroach or poet i
sat inside a mince pie
and laughed and laughed at
them myself the world seemed all
one golden glory boss
i came up the

street to get all this
wonderful stuff onto paper for
you but when i tried to
operate the typewriter
my foot would slip and
by the time i had control
of the machine again
the thoughts had gone
forever it is the
tragedy of the artist

                    archy

a close call

thank you boss for the
swiss cheese i hardly hoped
for a whole one i
took up quarters in it at once
the little galleries and caves and
runways appealed to
my sense of adventure after
i had made a square
meal i lay down in the inner

chamber for a nap feeling
safe i had hardly composed my limbs
for slumber when i heard
a gnawing sound and squeaks
of glee cautiously i
approached the north gallery a mouse
was there i hastily
retreated thinking i would make
my escape by way of one of the
windows on the south facade another
mouse was there the citadel
in short was attacked on all sides mice
mice mice coming nearer and nearer
their cold blooded squeaks and the champing
of their cruel teeth made the night
hideous minute after minute i lay
in the stokehold
until the slow minutes grew into
intolerable hours of agony great drops
of perspiration broke through the callus
on my brow i prayed for
dawn or the night watchman suddenly
into my retreat protruded a whisker it
was so near it tickled me closer and
closer it came it twitched i knew
that it had felt me a moment more and
all would be over just as

i prepared myself for another
transmigration mehitabel the cat
bounded into the room and i was saved
if you get me another cheese please
put a wire cage over it

                              archy

immorality

i was up to central
park yesterday watching some
kids build a snow man when
they were done and had
gone away i looked it
over they had used two
little chunks of wood for
the eyes i sat on one
of these and stared at
the bystanders along came a
prudish looking
lady from flatbush she
stopped and regarded the
snow man i stood

up on my hind legs in
the eye socket and
waved myself at her
horrors she cried even the
snow men in manhattan
are immoral officer arrest
that statue it winked
at me madam said the cop
accept the tribute
as a christmas present
and be happy my own
belief is that some
people have immorality
on the brain

                    archy

archy reports

ive got just one
resolution for this year boss
and here it is
better stuff and more rhymes
what have i got to look

forward to otherwise if
a vers libre poet is
reincarnated into
a cockroach what will
a vers libre cockroach
be reincarnated into i
ask you
i don t want to be
a amoeba next time do i
i sing the glad noo year
thats tending toward the norm
my song is one of cheer
im going to reform
see

                              archy

the demon rum

well boss on these
rainy days i wish i was
web footed like a jersey mosquito no
one has yet invented
an umbrella for cockroaches i was

pulled a piece of cheese rind over my head

over across the street
to the barroom you used to
frequent before you reformed today
and it was raining outside i
pulled a piece of cheese
rind over my head to
protect me from the weather and
started for the door as i
passed by one of the booths a man
who was sitting in it said to

his companion please call a
taxi for me where do you want to go
said his companion i am
bad again said the man i want to
go to some place where they
treat nervous diseases
at once you look all right
said his companion i may look all
right said he but i don t see
all right i just saw a piece
of cheese rind crawling along the
floor and as i passed by i
said to myself beware the demon rum
it gives your brain a quirk
it puts you on the bum
and gives the doctors work

                              archy

ancient lineage

professor slosson
says that the cockroach
is one of the eldest of the

creatures that inhabit
the globe
two hundred and fifty
millions of years
ago the cockroach
existed just as he exists
today of course it is
very flattering
to have this scientific
testimony to my ancient
lineage i can trace my
ancestry back without
a break to old adam cockroach
himself but the real question is
how much has the cockroach
learned in two hundred and
fifty million of years
well i can tell you
in a few brief words
the cockroach has learned
how to make man
the so called lord
of creation work for him
the cockroach lives
in peace and plenty
while the human race
hustles to support him

all the social institutions
of all time have existed
merely for the purpose
of forming a pyramid
on the apex of which
perches the cockroach triumphant
it has taken us a long
time but we point
with pride to the achievement
if you don t believe me
read professor slosson s
article

                    archy

the artist

i called on some friends in a
studio building the other evening and
while we were foraging about
for something to eat
we got caught on a
palette smeared over with all
the colors there are

leaping from this danger seven
or eight of us
landed upon an untouched canvas
that stood upon an easel
nearby waiting for the masters hand
and we walked across the
canvas on our way out of that
place it seems that we builded
better than we knew before
we could get to any safer place
than a spot behind a
gas radiator we heard human footsteps
approaching and an
instant later two men entered the
studio one of them switched on
the lights and the
other gave an exclamation of
pleasure and astonishment by jove
tommy he said to the owner of
the studio what is this new thing
of yours on the easel it is
the best thing you have done yet
i thought you were against
modernism and all
the new fangled stuff but i see
that you have come over to the new
school your style has

loosened up wonderfully old kid
i always said that if you
could only get away from the stiffness
and absurdity of the
conventional schools you had the
makings of a great painter in
you what do you call this
picture tommy
well said tommy with rare
presence of mind i have not
named it yet it is not altogether in
the newer mode you will observe i
have been struggling for a
compromise between the two methods
that would at the same time
allow me to express my
individuality on canvas i do
think myself that i have got more
freshness and directness into this
thing you have said his friend
it has the direct and naive approach
of the primitives and it
also has all that is
worthy to be retained of the
reticent sophistication of
the post pre raphaelites but what
do you say you are going to

call it it is said tommy as
you see a nocturne i have
been thinking of calling it
impressions of brooklyn
bridge in a fog and when his
friend went out he stood and looked at
the picture for a long time and
said now i wonder who in
hell slipped in here and did that it
is nothing short of genius could
i have done it myself when i
was drunk i must have done so
anyhow i will sign it and
taking up a brush he did so well i
stole a look at the canvas
myself and it looked like nothing
on earth to me but a canvas over
which a lot of cockroaches had
walked i may be a
critic but still i know what i
dont like yours for another
renaissance of the arts every
spring and every autumn

                              archy

destiny

well boss here i
am a cockroach still boss
i have often been disgusted
with life but now i am
even more disgusted
with death and transmigration i
would rather not inhabit
any body at all than
inhabit a cockroachs
body but it seems i
cant escape it that
is my destiny my doom my
punishment
when you struck me that
terrific blow a few
days ago and i
died there at
your feet my first
sensation was one of glad
relief what body will
the soul of archy transmigrate
into now i asked

myself will i go
higher in the scale of
life and inhabit the
body of a butterfly
or a dog or a
bird or will i sink
lower and go into the
carcase of a poison
spider or a politician
i sat on a blade of
grass and waited and wondered
what it would be i
hoped it wouldnt be
anything at all too soon
because if you remember
it was a hot
day and as i sat
on that blade of grass
in my naked soul and
let my feet hang over i
was deliciously
cool try it some of
these hot nights leave
your body in the
bed and go up on the
roof in your
spirit and float around

like a toy balloon its
great stuff well while
i was sitting there
thinking what i
would inhabit next if
it was up to me
personally i had
a swooning sensation
and when i came
to i was in the
flesh again dad gum
it i lifted first
one leg and then
another to see what i
was this time and
imagine my chagrin and
disappointment when i
found myself inside
another cockroach the
exact counterpart of the
one you smashed whats
the use of dying if
it dont get you
anywhere i was so
sore i went and
murdered a tumblebug i
suppose as a cockroach

i was not good enough
to be promoted
and not bad enough to
be set back boss a
thing like that makes a
fellow feel awful humble i
came back to town in
that special delivery letter i
would rather dodge
the thing
they cancel stamps with
all day than walk again
say boss
please thank my friends
for all the kind
words and flowers i
must close in haste there
is a new rat
in your office since i
was here last i
wish you would sprinkle a
little cereal in the
bottom of the waste paper
basket

                    archy

a discussion

there is a good deal
of metaphysical discussion going on
amongst my own little group here
i said freddy the rat was no
more he expired at the moment he
slew that tarantula well he had
once been a human and had
transmigrated into a rat just
as i had transmigrated into a
cockroach the question now
is where will freddy turn up next will
he go up or down the scale and
that has led to the further question as
to what is up and what is down
producing considerable dissension all the
spiders claim they are higher in
the scale than the cockroaches and that
lazy cat mehitabel looks on superciliously
as if confident that she has it on
all of us spiritually speaking
well all i have to say is that in
my case a soul got out of a vers libre

bard into a cockroach but i have
known cases which are exactly the
reverse if you get what i mean
not that i would name any names

archy

short course in natural history

you should be glad
you re not a tomcat
for when all is said
and done
you know youd hate
to pay insurance
on nine lives instead of one
be glad you re not
a centipede
you might your whole
ambition lose
if you had to find
the cash
to keep a centipede
in shoes
be glad you re not

a devilfish
if you had four pairs
of feet
what a trail
you d leave behind you
when you staggered
with the heat
                              archy

archy protests

well boss now youve got
your desk all cleaned up for the
first time since ive known you what
am i going to do for
a safe retreat in times of dire
need formerly i could crawl under a
bushel of poems and mehitabel the
cat could not find me this
room is as bare as the inside of
a drum you might at
least have left me a tobacco can i
feel as visible as a hyphen and not
half so sure of myself
                              archy

mehitabel sees it through

dear boss i met mehitabel
last night and asked her if
she did not think times were getting
a little better
she was digging for sustenance in a trash heap
at the moment and she looked as if
she might be a part of the heap herself
one of her legs has been damaged again
in a light with a rival in love
but she began to caper when i spoke to her
and replied as follows

good times and bad times
recoveries and depressions
wotthehell do i care
as long as somethings doing
when i lived on salmon
and oysters stewed in cream
i wasnt always happy
when i dug my scoffins
out of frozen garbage heaps
i wasnt always sad

economic problems
never tell the story
as far as im concerned
once i lived a fortnight
on moonlight wind and grass
and i danced every evening
with the shadows in the alley
and entertained my boy friends
with my melodious songs
wotthehell do i care
if the stomachs empty
when the spirits full
i have had my ups
and i have had my downs
but whether i was up
or whether i was down
there was something in my blood
that always set it dancing
and when the blood was jigging
the feet began to caper
some day i will voyage
on top a garbage scow
just a stiff dead feline
wreathed in orange peel and melon rinds
with shop worn salad garnished
down the bay theyll take me
to the dumping grounds

defunct as ancient nut shells
but wotthehell do i care
that day has not arrived
and good times or bad times
hard times or easy
there are three good feet
on old mehitabel
and she will keep them jigging
till the grim reaper slices
two more of them off

boss i think mehitabel is mistaken
about the milky way

and then she ll dance on one
till its frozen and resigns
and then her soul will caper
along the milky way
theres a dance or two in the old dame yet
and the word is toujours gai
boss i think mehitabel is mistaken
about the milky way
i think she is more like to dance
on hot cinders in the hereafter

                                    archy

mehitabel meets her mate

tis the right of a modern tabby to choose
the cats who shall father her kits
and its nice to be sure their pasts have been pure
and theyre free from fleas or fits

trial marriage i tried till i thoroughly tired
and i suffered somewhat from abduction
and my heart it was broken again and again
but twas excellent instruction

i always have been rather awesomely blest
with the instincts of a mother
and my life and my fate have been down to date
one kitten after another

triplets quadruplets quintuplets
in a most confusing succession
and it seems to keep up whether times are good
or wallowing in depression

and this is in spite of the terrible fact
i am not a real home body
but an artiste who views the domestic career
as damnably dull and shoddy

for i am a lady who has her whims
no tom cat holds my love
if i come to feel i have plighted my troth
to a little mauve turtle dove

but at last i have found my real romance
through the process of trial and error
and he is a ribald brute named bill
one eyed and a holy terror

his skull is ditched from a hundred fights
and he has little hair on his tail

but the son of a gun of a brindled hun
is indubitably male

over the fences we frolic and prance
under the blood red moon
and sing to the stars we are venus and mars
as we caper and clutch and croon

his good eye gleams like a coal of hell
from the murk of alley or yard
and the heart that jumps in the cage of his ribs
is hot and black and hard

says he as we rocket over the roofs
can you follow your limber bill
says i to him my demon slim
theres a dance in the old dame still

you pussies that purr on a persian rug
or mew to some fool for cream
little you know of the wild delight
of the outlaws midnight dream

a fish head filched from a garbage can
or a milk bottle raided at dawn
is better than safety and slavery
you punks that cuddle and fawn

you can stuff your bellies with oysters and shrimp
you may have your ribbon and bell
for bill and me it is liberty
o wotthehell bill wotthehell

says he to me old battle axe
you never was raised a pet
says i to willie i aint any lily
but theres pep in the old dame yet

last night when a bull pup gave us chase
bill turned and a rip of his claw
completely unseamed that slavering mutt
from his chin to his bloody jaw

we dance with the breeze of the summer nights
we dance with the winter sleet
with velvet paws on the velvet shadows
or whirl with frozen feet

we riot over the roof of the world
mehitabel and bill
you son of a gun of a brindled hun
theres a dance in the old dame still

mehitabel pulls a party

dear boss mehitabel shows
no evidences of reform
she flung a party in shinbone alley
last night and six of the toughest
tabbies i ever saw were her guests
all seven of them danced on the ash cans

she flung a party in shinbone alley

flirting their tails in the moonlight
and chanting as follows

oh wotthell do we care
if we are down and out
theres a dance or two in the old janes yet
so caper and swing about
up and down the alley
through and over the fence
for still we are attractive
to various feline gents
meow meow meow

now then sadie dont talk shady
try and remember you and myrtie
that you was raised a lady
that goes for you too gertie
oh i was chased down broadway
by a tom with a ribbon and bell
i says to him my limber jim
you seem to know me well
says he to me oh can it be
you are mehitabel
oh wotthell girls wotthell
as long as the gents is for us
we still got a job in the chorus
we aint no maltese flappers

we all seen better days
but we got as much it
as an ingenue kit
and it is the art that pays
meow meow meow

arch your back and caper
and kick at the golden moon
mebby some yeggs
who sell butter and eggs
will fling us a party soon
now then gertie dont get dirty
frankie frankie dont get cranky
and call any lowlife names
remember that you and your sister
were once society dames
and me and nance was debutants
before we was abducted
remember pearl that you was a girl
that a college went and instructed
dont chew the fat with no common cat
for you still got an honored place
oh climb the fence and caper
and kick the moon in the face

oh mebby we all are busted
oh mebby the winters are chill
but all of us girls seen better days

and we are ladies still
remember nell you was once a swell
you was raised a social pet
be careful sweet and act discreet
you may have come down in the world my dear
and you got a cauliflower
onto your ear
but you are a lady yet
meow meow meow

oh wotthell oh wotthell
as i came into the alley
i met a brindle swell
he says to me oh this can be
none but mehitabel
oh willie says i as i passed him by
you know me far too well
then cheerio my deario
prance and pirouette
as long as gents has such intents
theres life in the old world yet
meow meow meow

oh wotthell oh wotthell
i spy you brindle bill
come off the fence you feline gents
theres a dance in the old dame still
meow meow miaow

now then girls no shady jests
here come the gentlemen guests
you try and dance refined
remember you all was ladies born
and still are so inclined
now then sadie dont talk shady
or out you go on your nut
this aint any lousy harlem brawl
this aint any party in webster hall
we gotta recall we are nice girls all
and never was anything but
meow meow meow

                                        archy

not any proof

mehitabel the cat
tells me the feline
tribe were worshipped
in ancient egypt
and for that reason i
should hold her in more
respect

the feline tribe were worshipped in ancient egypt

well says i
minerva burst from
the head of jove
with a heluva yell
but that does not prove
that we should
stand in awe
of every case of
mastoiditis

archy

statesmanship

i was talking
with an insect the
other day about the
hard times that
cockroaches have to
get a living every
mans hand is against them
and occasionally his
foot meals
are few and far between
why in the world
says this
insect do you not
go to the country and become
grasshoppers if
living in town and being
cockroaches is getting
too difficult for you
i was astonished
at the simplicity of the
solution but as i
thought it over it occurred

go to the country and become grasshoppers

to me that
perhaps it sounded more
statesmanlike than it
really was
how i asked him are
cockroaches to become
grasshoppers
that is a mere
detail he said which i
leave to you for

solution i have outlined
the general scheme for your
salvation so do not ask
me to settle the mere
details i trust to you for
that you must do
something for yourself
we philosophers cannot do it all
for you unaided you
must learn self help
but alas i fear that
your inherent stupidity will
balk all efforts
to improve your condition
boss i offer you
this little story
for what it is worth
if you are able to
find in it something
analogous to a number
of easy schemes
for the improvement of the
human race you
may do immense good by
printing it
yours for reform
                              archy

the author s desk

i climbed upon my boss his desk
to type a flaming ballad
and there i found a heap grotesque
of socks and songs and salad

some swedenborgian dope on hell
with modernistic hunches
remnants of plays that would not jell
and old forgotten lunches

a plate once flushed with pride and pie
now chill with pallid verses
a corkless jug of ink hard by
sobbed out its life with curses

six sad bedraggled things lay there
inertly as dead cats
three sexless rhymes that could not pair
and three discouraged spats

the feet of song be tender things
like to the feet of waiters

and need when winter bites and stings
sesquipedalian gaiters

peter the pup sprawled on the heap
disputing all approaches
or growled and grumbled in his sleep
or waked and snapped at roaches

i found a treatise on the soul
which bragged it undefeated
and a bill for thirteen tons of coal
by fate left unreceipted

books on the modern girl s advance
wrapped in a cutey sark
with honi soit qui mal y pense
worked for its laundry mark

mid broken glass the spider slinks
while memories stir and glow
of olden happy far off drinks
and bottles long ago

such is the litter at the root
of song and story rising
or noisome pipe or cast off boot
feeding and fertilizing

as lilies burgeon from the dirt
into the golden day
dud epic and lost undershirt
survive times slow decay

still burrowing far and deep i found
a razor coldly soapy
and at the center of the mound
some most surprising opi

some modest pages chaste and shy
for pocket poke or sporran
written by archy published by
doubleday and doran

                    archy the cockroach

what the ants are saying

dear boss i was talking with an ant
the other day
and he handed me a lot of
gossip which ants the world around
are chewing over among themselves

i pass it on to you
in the hope that you may relay it to other
human beings and hurt their feelings with it
no insect likes human beings
and if you think you can see why
the only reason i tolerate you is because
you seem less human to me than most of them
here is what the ants are saying

it wont be long now it wont be long
man is making deserts of the earth
it wont be long now
before man will have used it up
so that nothing but ants
and centipedes and scorpions
can find a living on it
man has oppressed us for a million years
but he goes on steadily
cutting the ground from under
his own feet making deserts deserts deserts

we ants remember
and have it all recorded
in our tribal lore
when gobi was a paradise
swarming with men and rich
in human prosperity

it is a desert now and the home
of scorpions ants and centipedes

what man calls civilization
always results in deserts
man is never on the square
he uses up the fat and greenery of the earth
each generation wastes a little more
of the future with greed and lust for riches

north africa was once a garden spot
and then came carthage and rome
and despoiled the storehouse
and now you have sahara
sahara ants and centipedes

toltecs and aztecs had a mighty
civilization on this continent
but they robbed the soil and wasted nature
and now you have deserts scorpions ants
        and centipedes
and the deserts of the near east
followed egypt and babylon and assyria
and persia and rome and the turk
the ant is the inheritor of tamerlane
and the scorpion succeeds the caesars

america was once a paradise
of timberland and stream
but it is dying because of the greed
and money lust of a thousand little kings
who slashed the timber all to hell
and would not be controlled
and changed the climate
and stole the rainfall from posterity
and it wont be long now
it wont be long
till everything is desert
from the alleghenies to the rockies
the deserts are coming
the deserts are spreading
the springs and streams are drying up
one day the mississippi itself
will be a bed of sand
ants and scorpions and centipedes
shall inherit the earth

men talk of money and industry
of hard times and recoveries
of finance and economics
but the ants wait and the scorpions wait
for while men talk they are making deserts all
       the time
getting the world ready for the conquering ant

drought and erosion and desert
because men cannot learn

rainfall passing off in flood and freshet
and carrying good soil with it
because there are no longer forests
to withhold the water in the
billion meticulations of the roots

it wont be long now it won't be long
till earth is barren as the moon
and sapless as a mumbled bone

dear boss i relay this information
without any fear that humanity
will take warning and reform

archy